The Phonology and Morphology of Reduplication

Studies in Generative Grammar 52

Editors

Harry van der Hulst
Jan Koster
Henk van Riemsdijk

Mouton de Gruyter
Berlin · New York

The Phonology and Morphology of Reduplication

by

Eric Raimy

Mouton de Gruyter
Berlin · New York 2000

Mouton de Gruyter (formerly Mouton, The Hague)
is a Division of Walter de Gruyter GmbH & Co. KG, Berlin.

The series Studies in Generative Grammar was formerly published by
Foris Publications Holland.

♾ Printed on acid-free paper which falls within the guidelines
of the ANSI to ensure permanence and durability.

Library of Congress Cataloging-in-Publication Data

Raimy, Eric.
   The phonology and morphology of reduplication / by Eric Raimy.
       p.   cm. − (Studies in generative grammar ; 52)
   Includes bibliographical references and index.
   ISBN 3 11 016932 0 (cloth : alk. paper)
   1. Grammar, Comparative and general − Reduplication.
   2. Grammar, Comparative and general − Phonology.   3. Grammar, Comparative and general − Morphology. I. Title. II. Series.
   P245 .R347 2000
   415−dc21   00-053304

Die Deutsche Bibliothek − Cataloging-in-Publication Data

Raimy, Eric:
   The phonology and morphology of reduplication / by Eric Raimy. −
   Berlin ; New York : Mouton de Gruyter, 2000
     (Studies in generative grammar ; 52)
     ISBN 3-11-016932-0

Printing & Binding: Hubert & Co., Göttingen.
Cover design: Christopher Schneider, Berlin.
Printed in Germany.

Acknowledgements

This book is an outgrowth of my dissertation that I wrote at the University of Delaware. All of my thanks from that project are carried over to this one too. Additional thanks for helping with the revisions of my dissertation that resulted in this book are as follows.

Bill Idsardi has helped with every aspect of this book from long discussions of its contents to helping proofread and copy edit the final version. Without Bill's input this project would not have reached the level of sucess it has attained. John Frampton, Morris Halle, and Charles Reiss have all been supportive of the ideas here from their first incarnation and I thank them for showing their interest and arguing with me about various points. Their arguments have improved particular analyses in this book greatly but they do not necessarily agree with everything that I say. Donna Jo Napoli encouraged me to publish this work as a book so her role here can not be underestimated. The feedback from audiences at the 2000 Montreal-Ottawa-Toronto Phonology Workshop, New York University, and the University of Pennsylvania has also helped shape the present analyses. Finally, I would like to thank my wife Bonnie who has spent too much time alone while I was revising and paying attention to this book. Her support allows me to persevere through long projects like this.

Contents

Chapter 1
Introduction

The aim of this book is to present, illustrate and defend a representational theory of reduplication. The main insight of the approach developed here is that reduplication is the repetition of a sequence of segments. A novel representation for reduplication arises from the clarification of precedence information in morpho-phonological representations, resulting in the possibility of loops as in (1).

(1)# → k → æ → t → % = [kætkæt]

The beginning and end of the loop act like ‖: and :‖ in musical notation in marking off the material that is repeated. The beginning and end of a representation is marked by # (the beginning) and % (the end) in (1). Since the loop encompasses the entire segmental content of (1) total reduplication results.

The motivation for this work is that reduplication has become a central issue for much current research on phonological theory. The title of this book, *The phonology and morphology of reduplication*, indicates both the general goals of this work and how the approach to reduplication presented here departs from most present analyses in placing an emphasis on the representation of reduplication within the morpho-phonology. The most fruitful analysis of reduplication as a phenomenon unto itself will utilize aspects of both phonology and morphology and any analysis that neglects either of these areas will not fully illuminate what reduplication is.

One of the first questions that should be asked of any analysis of reduplication is how the analysis contributes to the areas of phonology and morphology. McCarthy and Prince (1993b, 1995) claim that reduplication provides a blueprint for all of phonology since reduplication provides fundamental insights into correspondence theory (McCarthy and Prince 1995). It is obvious what reduplication contributes to the study of phonology for those who subscribe to this view. Reduplication is a microcosm of phonology and all aspects of phonological processes can be studied and illuminated by work on reduplication patterns.

The view of reduplication in this book differs drastically from the one offered by McCarthy and Prince. Reduplication will be shown to result from general properties of phonology and morphology and more specifically to be the result of the interaction between these two modules of grammar. A modular approach allows the morphological and phonological aspects of reduplication to be accounted for within separate components using module-general principles. An explanation of reduplication specific processes will result from the special phonological structures that are created in the morphology and interpreted by the phonology. Consequently, the special behavior in reduplicated structures first identified by Wilbur (1973) and used as primary arguments for correspondence theory by McCarthy and Prince (1995) do not require any sort of special mechanism. These effects are derived from the representations for reduplication proposed in this work and by a modular approach to grammar. This result is the most important contribution to phonological theory that the study of reduplication in this book provides. No previous model of reduplication has been able to account for the phonological behavior of reduplication without resorting to reduplication specific mechanisms. The lack of reduplication specific mechanisms is one of the strongest arguments in favor of the analysis of reduplication presented in the following chapters.

Deriving the special phonological behavior of reduplication in the phonology module has important implications for phonology in general. The main consequence is that certain aspects of phonological representations have to be revised. Specifically, the representation of precedence in phonology is made explicit in this theory and it turns out that a greater variety of precedence structures can be represented than previously contemplated. Allowing novel precedence structures in the phonology requires present ideas on what triggers a rule to be rethought and refined. The interaction between the new types of possible precedence structures and refinements in what triggers a rule provides the explanation for the surface exceptional behavior of some phonological rules in reduplicated structures. These surface apparent exceptions to phonological rules turn out to be simple cases of opacity which are accounted for and predicted by a derivational model of phonology. These points about phonology will be fully outlined in chapter 2 but a short summary of those results is that once the proper revisions to phonological theory have been made, reduplication is in no way exceptional from a phonological point of view. The behavior of phonological rules in reduplicative structures follows from general principles of phonology. The contribution of reduplication to the understanding of phonology is that certain types of precedence structures only regularly appear in reduplicated forms and thus we must look to reduplication to explicate some (but not all) aspects of phonology. Reduplication is not a microcosm of phonology, it is a morphological construction that provides a complex phonological representation that illuminates previously uninvestigated aspects of phonological theory. Reduplication is not the exception to generative phonology, it is the proof of generative phonology.

Reduplication provides analogous insights into morphological theory. Previous approaches to reduplication (Carrier 1979, Marantz 1982) treat it as a special kind of morphological process and this weakens the otherwise substantial insights that these approaches have provided. Work by Carrier (1979) argues that reduplication is best understood by treating it as a transformational rule (as in Chomsky 1965) that resides in the morphological component. Placing part of reduplication in the morphological component is an insight that is retained in the present approach. The transformational approach to reduplication, though, is costly because of the brute-force power allowed in that approach. Also, with the changes in syntactic theory, reduplication would be the only grammatical construction that would require that type of generative apparatus and this highlights the special treatment of reduplication in this approach. Proposals by Marantz (1982) (based on McCarthy 1979) treat reduplication as special kind of affixation that triggers a melodic copying process. That analysis and the resulting revisions that refined what kind of phonological structure is actually affixed (from

CV slots to the "authentic units of prosody" in McCarthy and Prince 1986) all have the flaw that the additional melodic copying process is stipulated and does not follow from any principle. One can easily imagine an alternative where default vowels and consonants fill out the template. That is, Marantz's approach does not really explain why reduplication exists in natural languages. This aspect of affix and copy approaches to reduplication prevents reduplication from being collapsed with general affixation (Anderson 1992:60).

Reduplication is a *readjustment process* (Halle and Marantz 1993,1994) in the present work. This result is obtained through the novel precedence structures that can be accommodated in the phonology. Affixation as a general process concatenates some phonological structure with another phonological structure. Part of concatenation is specifying how the affix is to be joined with the base. Does the affix come before the base? After the base? After and before the base? This last option is how a loop is constructed in a base that results in reduplication. Consider the informal examples of prefixation, suffixation and reduplication in (2).

(2)   a. un-   /ʌ → n → "before"/
       un-lock   *lock-un

       b. -er   /"after" → ə → r/
       lock-er   *er-lock

       c. -schm-   / 'after' → ʃ → m → 'before'/
       lock-schm-ock   *schm-ock-lock   *lock-lock-schm

       d. # → l → a → k → %

(2a) shows the case of a prefix and an inherent aspect of the representation of a prefix is that it precedes the base that it concatenates to. (2b) shows a suffix which is identical to a prefix except that it follows the base that it concatenates to. (2c) shows a case of reduplication in English where *schm-* causes reduplication and replaces part of the repeated word. Crucially, the repetition is caused because of the requirement to be both "after" and "before" the base which causes a loop to be created which is shown in (2d). Formalization of the concatenation of affixes and readjustments to bases that result in reduplication is presented in chapter 3.

Once the resemblance between prefixation, suffixation and reduplication is recognized, reduplication only differs from other forms of affixation in the type of precedence relationship (i.e. "before", "after", "inside" to create infixes) between the two concatenated phonological structures. The types of possible precedence relationships in affixation create a typology of affixes that covers prefixation, suffixation, infixation and reduplicative templates from a simple set of parameters that specify where an affix will attach to a base. A similar proposal has been made by Anderson (1992:210) on where infixation can be placed so there appears to be a convergence on this point between other work and the proposals made here.

The common thread between the contributions to both phonological and morphological theories that the analysis of reduplication developed here is that reduplication becomes a well understood phenomenon that results from the general architecture of these particular grammatical modules. No reduplication specific mechanisms are required and in a certain sense reduplication is predicted to exist as a very common feature in human language.

Providing an explanation for reduplication is a large claim to make and the following chapters of this book show how and why this goal is achieved. Chapter 2 investigates the phonological aspects of reduplication. One of the most important findings in this chapter is that reduplication does not require parallel computation that McCarthy and Prince (1995) argue for. The presence of intermediate representations are crucial to understanding the difference between the "normal" application of phonological rules and "over" and "under" application in the sense of Wilbur (1973). The representations employed here to accomplish an analysis of the interaction between phonological rules and reduplication are novel because they introduce explicit representation of precedence relations among phonological segments. This formal clarification of phonological representations provides the crucial phonological environments that explain the interaction between phonological rules and reduplicated structures. The fit between the revised representations and the empirical behavior of reduplicated structures is a strong indication that this approach provides a deep understanding of the phonological behavior of reduplication in general.

Another aspect of phonological theory that is investigated in chapter 2 is the role of linearization in phonology. The idea that there is a linearization process that ensures representations will meet bare output conditions (Chomsky 1995) has been a tenet of minimalist approaches in syntax since Kayne (1994). I propose that phonological representations must also meet this bare output condition but that linearization in phonology differs from that in syntax. Syntactic linearization maps syntactic hierarchical structures into linear sequences of elements while phonological linearization ensures that sequences of elements are interpretable at the motor/perceptual interface. An interesting aspect of the linearization process in the phonological component is that it has the character of an optimization process where fixed language universal principles of economy determine a mapping between an input representation and a necessarily asymmetrical output representation. While asymmetry plays a central role in both syntactic linearization and phonological linearization, these two processes appear to be distinct. Identifying language universal characteristics of linearization in phonology will be another contribution of the present approach to general phonological theory.

Chapter 3 examines the morphological aspects of reduplication. The revisions to phonological theory proposed in chapter 2 will allow a purely "item" based morphological analysis of reduplication. Several morphological analyses of reduplication patterns based on the grammatical model of Distributed Morphology (Halle and Marantz 1993, 1994) will be presented. Distributed Morphology (like Chomsky and Halle 1968) posits an independent level of morphological representation that precedes the phonological component. The morphological component exchanges morphosyntactic features for vocabulary items that consist of phonological material. Reduplicative morphemes specify a vocabulary item that triggers a readjustment which creates a loop in the temporal structure of a previously spelled out vocabulary item.

A basic typology that distinguishes roots from affixes and between different types of affixes exists due to the differing types of precedence information that is present in a vocabulary item. Roots consist of vocabulary items that have both a specified beginning and end. Affixes have a variable in the place of their beginning, ending or both as part of the vocabulary item. The setting of a variable that appears in a vocabulary item determines whether the item is a prefixal, suffixal, infixal or reduplicative in nature.

Another reflex of variables used to define precedence relations is that templates in reduplication that have been previously used as evidence in favor of Prosodic Morphology (McCarthy and Prince 1986, 1993b) are derived without any reference to an output goal or surface representation. The variables that produce the different reduplicative templates are similar in form to ones required to describe the placement of infixes and resemble proposals made by Anderson (1992) on where infixed affixes may appear.

The contribution to the understanding of the morphological aspects of reduplication and morphology in general are readily apparent from the broad ranging effects of the revisions to phonological representations proposed in chapter 2. The goal of removing templates from phonological theory first proposed by McCarthy and Prince (1994b) is achieved in chapter 3 without dispersing or transferring the structural information inherent in a template to other parts of the phonology.

Chapter 4 identifies three theoretical issues that distinguish present proposals on reduplication from previous ones that have recurred throughout previous analyses of reduplication. These issues identify the inadequacies of previous approaches to reduplication and indicate what an adequate model of reduplication must account for. The proposals in chapters 2 and 3 do not suffer from the any of the inadequacies identified and appear to have all of the qualities of an adequate model of reduplication. Finally, chapter 4 summarizes the findings of this book and indicates future directions for research. As with any proposal of substance, many questions that go beyond the topics discussed in this book are generated. Even with the large amount of recent work on reduplication many of these questions are empirical in nature and can only be answered through more research utilizing the representations proposed here. In the end, it is the representational proposals in this work that are the most important contribution to generative grammar and these representations can be utilized by models of grammar different from the one assumed in this book. Not all results achieved here are available to non-derivational models of grammar though and this point indicates that reduplication provides general empirical arguments in favor of a derivational model of grammar.

Chapter 2
The phonology of reduplication

The theory of reduplication developed here takes strong positions on two issues: the nature of phonological identity and the relationship between morphology and phonology. Phonological identity will be minimal in that only *self-identity* will be necessary in order to account for backcopying effects in reduplication. Self-identity in this sense means that a segment or feature is only identical to itself and that there is no mediating function such as *correspondence* (McCarthy and Prince 1995) that instantiates a relationship of identity between two phonologically distinct entities. The relationship between morphology and phonology will also be strong in that the phonology receives an impoverished representation to operate on from a separate morphology module. These characteristics provide a strong indication that the model presented here is adequate in accounting for reduplication without process specific mechanisms.

The central aspect of the model of reduplication that will be developed in this and the following chapter is a formalization of explicit precedence in phonological representations. We will begin by discussing how and why explicit precedence should be represented in phonology. Once this issue is settled, we begin to investigate some of the more complex phonological structures that can be built within the revised view of precedence in phonology and how these representations can be utilized in accounting for reduplication. The final section of this chapter discusses how the notion of a derivation allows this model of reduplication to provide an explanation for all aspects of interaction between reduplication and phonological rules.

2.1 Precedence in phonology

It is often sufficient to consider phonological representations as simple strings of segments. That is, in most works (Chomsky 1975 and Sproat 1985 being two notable exceptions), linear precedence in phonological representations is implicitly represented by left-to-right spatial orientation in visual diagrams. Accordingly, we have phonological representations like those found in (3). In (3) and following, # is used to explicitly indicate the beginning of the string and % to indicate the end, eliminating any possible ambiguity from the standard use of # alone.

(3)   a. #kæt%
       b. #tæk%

Given (3), we are to understand that in (3a) "# precedes k", "k precedes æ", "æ precedes t" and "t precedes %" where both # and % represent null sets so "# precedes k" is actually understood as "nothing precedes k" and "t precedes %" is "t precedes nothing". (3b) contrasts with (3a) in that it has the opposite precedence relationships in that "# precedes t", "t precedes æ", "æ precedes k" and "k precedes %" are all true. The difference between these two forms is not based on any segmental information. It is based solely on the ordering of the segments and nothing else.

Following from the assumptions about how precedence is encoded in representations like (3), we can see that the relation of precedence in phonological representations such as (3) is asymmetrical, transitive and irreflexive. Precedence is asymmetrical because if "k precedes æ" in a form then "æ precedes k" is necessarily false if there are only unique instances of these segments. Precedence is transitive because "k precedes t" is true since "k precedes æ" and "æ precedes t" are also true.[1] Finally, precedence is irreflexive because there is no way of encoding the idea that a segment precedes itself[2] in this type of representation.

Sagey (1990) claims that these characteristics of precedence in phonological representations result from real world knowledge present in the phonology. Representations that do not have these characteristics are ill-formed because they violate conditions of the real world, not because of some requirement posited in Universal grammar. This allows Sagey to remove all well-formedness conditions on the model of feature geometry that she posits.

Sagey's point about real world knowledge determining possible precedence structures receives new insight when combined with Chomsky's (1995) bare output conditions. The nature of the phonetics motor control interface should be sufficient to characterize the limits on possible precedence structures without having to posit real world knowledge in a cognitive model. That is, the motor system has to be at least minimally adapted to real-world facts about time and temporal relations, but does *phonology* need be?

The question now is what kind of bare output condition does phonology have with respect to precedence structures. On this point, I think Sagey is correct in that phonological representations must be asymmetrical, transitive and irreflexive in the phonetics module. This position entails that precedence be explicitly represented in phonological representations. If precedence is not explicitly represented it can not be determined if a structure is well-formed or not.

With the idea of explicit representation in mind, now consider the representations in (4).

(4)   a. # → k → æ → t → %
       b. % ← t ← æ ← k ← #
       c. % ← k ← æ ← t ← #

If the symbol → is used to represent the relationship of *precedes* then (4a) and (4b) are equivalent because both representations have the following precedence relationships: "# precedes k", "k precedes æ", "æ precedes t" and "t precedes %". (4c) is different from (4a) and (4b) since the overall ordering of the form is that "# precedes t", "t precedes æ", "æ precedes k" and "k precedes %". The addition of a precedence symbol makes explicit the precedence relationships in phonological representations usually only implicit from left-to-right graphic ordering. By changing the implicit representation into an explicit one, we can now more fully explore its characteristics as we can develop the theoretical constructs and vocabulary so as to make our definitions more precise.

Phonological representations that have non-asymmetrical[3] and non-irreflexive characteristics can now be contemplated. These characteristics are not necessarily aberrant; they simply express novel phonological structures that may provide important insights into various phenomena. One of the claims of this chapter is that these novel phonological representations provide insights into the nature of reduplication. Consider an example of total reduplication from Indonesian in (5).

(5)   a. $\# \rightarrow b \rightarrow u \rightarrow k \rightarrow u \rightarrow \%$ [buku]
      b. $\# \rightarrow b \rightarrow u \rightarrow k \rightarrow u \rightarrow \%$ [buku-buku]

(5a) is the unreduplicated form and it resembles a "traditional" phonological representation that respects the characteristics of asymmetry, irreflexivity and transitivity. (5b) represents a reduplicated form and the distinct part of this representation is that it contains a "loop". The looping nature of (5b) causes this representation to be non-asymmetrical and non-irreflexive but the characteristic of transitivity remains.

Transitivity is a basic characteristic of phonological representations because the ordering of segments is an arbitrary fact of a phonological representation. Attempting to derive the ordering of segments in the phonology is futile because in all languages [kæt] ≠ [tæk]. It is thus obvious, that there are non-trivial and non-derivable ordering relationships between segments in the phonology and in order to fully interpret phonological representations these relationships must be present throughout the phonological derivation.

The main claim of this chapter is that reduplication is looping. The graph representation in (5b) allows phonological representations to contain loops, a characteristic that could not be expressed in previous frameworks. Following from this claim is the idea that the non-asymmetry that is introduced by the loop *is the cause* of the repetition of material in the phonetic form that listeners recognize as reduplication. Repetition is caused by loops in phonological representations because of a linearization process that is present within the phonology. Since we are assuming that the phonetics module imposes bare output conditions of transitivity, asymmetricality and irreflexivity on the phonology module there must be some way of

ensuring that a phonological representation meets these requirements at the phonetics-phonology interface. Otherwise, the phonetics module would not be able to interpret the phonological
representation.

The idea of a linearization process in phonology is not completely new. Single melody models of reduplication (Mester 1988,
Uhrbach 1987) require a linearization process that creates a well-
formed single prosodic structure from the dual prosodic structure of
a reduplicated form. This particular linearization process owes its
roots to the idea of tier conflation originally proposed in McCarthy
(1979). The linearization process utilized in this model of reduplication specifically ensures that representations output from this
process are asymmetric and irreflexive[4] while at the same time pre-
serving the precedence information that is encoded in the graph representations. To preserve precedence information in a looping
structure, the segments that are within the loop are *repeated*.

Linearization in phonology appears to be an optimization process that attempts to follow certain characteristics. Two inviolable
characteristics of this process are that the output representation
must be asymmetrical and no new precedence relationships are
added during linearization. Only precedence relations that are present in the input representation may be present in the output. The
other goals (sometimes incompletely obtained) of linearization are
to use morphologically added material before lexical material and
to generate the shortest possible output.

Formatives that contain loops have non-asymmetrical structure
that must be made asymmetrical somehow. The linearization process repeats segments in order to create an asymmetrical precedence
structure from a non-asymmetrical one. Consider the reduplicated
form from the Indonesian example in (5) repeated below in (6)
along with possible linearized forms.

(6)   a. $\# \to b \to u \to k \to u \to \%$

   b. $\# \to b \to u \to k \to u \to b \to u \to k \to u \to \%$
   c. $\# \to b \to u \to k \to u \to \%$
   d. $\# \to b \to u \to k \to u \to b \to u \to k \to u \to b \to u \to k \to u \to \%$

(6a) presents the reduplicated form that must be linearized in order to remove the non-asymmetrical relations within its precedence structure. (6b) is the occurring linearized form and we see that every link is used at least once and the lexical links have been used a second time as a result of using the morphological link from /u/ to /b/ (indicated by the dashed link in [6]). Note that linearization resembles the containment model presented in Prince and Smolensky (1993) in that no new precedence relations can be added. This limits the computation that is required by the linearization process (Idsardi and Raimy 2000). (6c) presents an output that has not used all the precedence links in the input form and more importantly a morphological link was not used. Linearization places a priority on utilizing morphologically added links and there are cases where the use of a morphological link prevents the use of a lexical link. This occurs in the analysis of Temiar presented in chapter 3. Finally, (6d) presents an output that repeats more segments and precedence links than (6b) but does not contain any links or segments that are not in (25b). This output is rejected because it violates an economy condition. Consequently, other outputs like *buku-buku-buku-buku*, *buku-buku-buku-buku-buku*, etc. that contain gratuitous repetition of phonological material are not produced by the linearization process because these are not the most economical outputs possible.

Moravcsik (1978) provides empirical support for the economization aspect of the linearization process where each loop produces only one repetition of material. In this extensive survey of reduplication patterns found in the world's languages, no pattern of reduplication is found that does not have a specific number of repetitions of segmental material. Most of the patterns that are cited only repeat once, but patterns of double reduplication (e.g. Lushootseed, Urbanczyk 1996) do occur. Patterns of double reduplication are caused by the presence of more than one reduplicative morpheme resulting in multiple loops. The crucial point here is that the number of times a section of segmental material is repeated is not arbitrary, or random. It is fully under the control of the grammar.

The representational approach to reduplication presented here immediately provides solutions to the issues that have plagued previous models of reduplication. If reduplication is a loop, then reduplicative morphemes are reduced to a purely phonological representation without requiring any additional copying mechanism or correspondence functions. This allows reduplication to be accounted by the general architecture of grammar without resorting to any process specific mechanism. Linearization is not specific to reduplication because it ensures that the bare output condition of asymmetry is met by all phonological representations. In chapter 3, we will see that infixes also produce complex precedence structures where the output of linearization is a different precedence structure from the input so it is readily apparent that overt linearization effects are not limited to reduplication.

Since there is nothing process specific in reduplication in this representational model, the insight that reduplication is nothing more than affixation provided by Marantz (1982) is fully implemented. Reduplicative morphemes consist minimally of a precedence relationship that creates a loop in the temporal structure of the base. Prespecification effects indicate that reduplicative morphemes can contain segmental material of their own along the loop and it is only the specification of the precedence relationships of a morpheme that cause it to be reduplicative. These morphological aspects of reduplication will be discussed in much greater detail in chapter 3.

The other main benefit of the graph theoretic approach to reduplication is that a phonological analysis of backcopying effects is available without resorting to a transderivational mechanism. We will turn to this topic in the next section.

2.2   Reduplication and phonological rules

The revision of precedence information present in phonological representations proposed in the previous section creates novel structures that provide insight into the interaction between reduplication and phonological rules. This section will present case studies of the interaction of reduplication and phonological rules that show how these novel structures properly describe the observed interactions. The particular languages included in this section were selected primarily due to claims that derivational models of reduplication are incapable of providing a conceptually adequate analysis of these particular data. Each of the case studies refutes these claims because the data are accounted for simply and completely. Thus, all of these case studies provide strong evidence in support of the model of reduplication presented here.

2.2.1 Remarks on backcopying

Raimy (2000) presents analyses of Malay and Akan to refute the claims made by McCarthy and Prince (1995) that a derivational model of reduplication is conceptually unable to account for backcopying effects in reduplication. The basic aspects of the analyses of Malay and Akan will be presented in order to facilitate the case studies in the following sections. I refer the reader to Raimy (2000) for the full details of these particular analyses.

Malay presents a clear case of backcopying. The data in (7) show that nasalization spreads rightward in Malay. Nasality is spread from a nasal segment to all following vowels and oral obstruents block this process. The backcopying of nasal features is seen in the reduplicated forms in (7) since the vowels in the word initial syllables are nasalized in places that are not transparently preceded by a nasal segment (Onn 1980, Kenstowicz 1981).

(7) a. hamã   'germ'   hãmã-hãmã   'germs'
     b. waɲĩ   'fragrant'   wãɲĩ-wãɲĩ   'fragrant (intens.)'
     c. aŋăn   'reverie'   ăŋăn-ăŋăn   'ambition'
     d. aŋĕn   'wind'   ăŋĕn-ăŋĕn   'unconfirmed news'

Pursuing the claim that reduplication is looping, (7d) must have the representation in (8).

(8) $\# \rightarrow a \rightarrow \eta \rightarrow e \rightarrow n \rightarrow \%$

Given the representation in (8), the /a/ is preceded by both # and /n/. Thus, /a/ is preceded by a nasal segment though that is not the only thing that precedes it. Once this aspect of the representation is realized, the behavior of nasal spread in Malay reduplicated forms is no longer surprising. Given this representation, it is expected as long as having a nasal before a vowel is sufficient to trigger nasalization.

Seong (1994) posits the nasal spread rule in (9) to account for the nasal spread process in Malay. (The arrow between the C and V is the precedence link.)

(9)

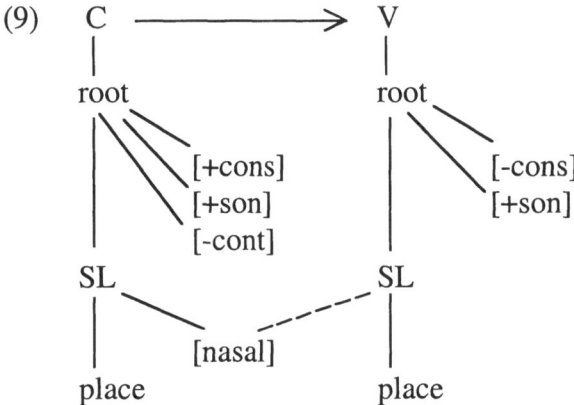

To complete the formulation of this rule, we must also specify that this rule is iterative (Archangeli and Pulleyblank 1994).

The question that must now be addressed is whether the rule in (9) should apply in the representation in (8). The /e/ that follows /ŋ/ should clearly be nasalized because it is in an environment that triggers the rule in (9). The more important question is whether the word initial /a/ should also be nasalized. Because of the addition of the precedence link from /n/ to /a/ caused by the reduplicative morpheme, the word initial vowel appears in two distinct environments at the same time. /a/ is in both a word initial environment [# → a] and a postnasal environment [n → a]. Is this situation sufficient to cause the nasal spread rule to apply?

The empirical facts (for the Penang dialect) indicate that the nasal spread rule in Malay does apply in this case. (10) shows which segments have the feature [nasal] in the reduplicated structure before and after the application of the nasal spread rule. The dotted line indicates spreading of a feature in (10b).

(10) a.   [nasal]   [nasal]   b.   [nasal]

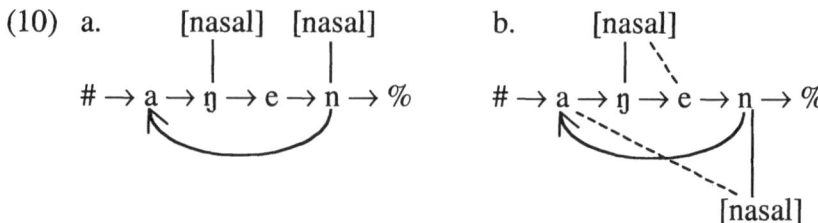

(10b) shows that the nasal spread rule spreads nasal from /ŋ/ to /e/ and from /n/ to /a/. Later (10b) will be linearized producing the form in (11).

(11)   [nasal]

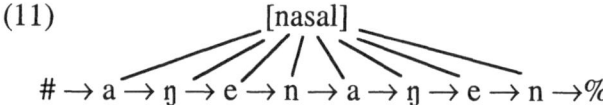

(11) assumes that the two nasal features in (10b) have been fused into a single one as part of the linearization process which economizes all aspects of the representation, not just precedence information. This fusion of [nasal] is not a required feature of this analysis so an alternative form of (11) might retain two (or three) separate [nasal] features. This does not affect the present analysis.

With an analysis of backcopying in Malay in hand, let us turn to Akan. This example of underapplication and surface normal application of a rule in a reduplicated form is important because it presents a case where a phonological rule behaves differently from the nasal spread rule in Malay.

McCarthy and Prince (1995:340-345) present the interaction of palatalization and reduplication in Akan as a case of underapplication of a phonological process. This example is interesting because palatalization does occur in some reduplicative forms. The prediction of when the palatalization rule should underapply and when it should apply normally is the issue at hand.

McCarthy and Prince (1995:341) follow Schachter and Fromkin (1968) in claiming that Akan shows a process of palatalization[5] where [dorsal] segments are prohibited from preceding non-low front vowels (i/ı or e/ɛ). The data in (12) support this position.

(12) ʨɛ   *kɛ   'divide'
     ʥe   *ge   'receive'
     ɥi   *wi   'nibble'
     çı   *hı   'border'
     ɲɥĩn   *ŋwın   'weave'

Dorsal segments that are present in Akan (k, g, w and ŋʷ) and /h/ usually do not precede a non-low front vowel. McCarthy and Prince claim that this is due to a process that spreads [coronal] from the vowel onto the preceding [dorsal] segment.

Some reduplicated forms violate this generalization because both [dorsal] segments and /h/ can appear before non-low front vowels.

(13) kı-kaʔ   *ʨı-kaʔ   *ʨı-ʨaʔ   'bite'
     hı-hawʔ   *çı-hawʔ   *çı-çawʔ   'trouble'

This particular pattern of reduplication in Akan is CV with the V being prespecified for the feature [high] and it receives its value for [back] from the following vowel.[6] Since we are interested in the palatalization process, we will only be looking at reduplicated forms with non-back vowels. In order to facilitate discussion, I will notate the vowel in the reduplicant as /ı/. This will allow us to focus on the question as to why this vowel does not trigger palatalization.

CV reduplication with a prespecified vowel can be represented as the addition of the prespecified vowel with precedence links to and from the word initial consonant. This approach produces the representation in (14).

(14) $\# \rightarrow k \rightarrow a \rightarrow ʔ \rightarrow \%$

Given the representation in (14), we must now formulate the palatalization rule. McCarthy and Prince (1995) propose that palatalization is the result of spreading [coronal] from the non-low front vowel onto the [dorsal] segment creating a complex palatal segment. Using this suggestion, we can formulate this rule as in (15).

(15)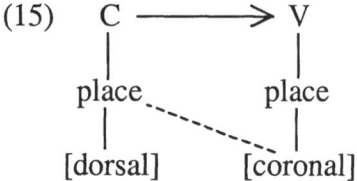

Considering the Malay example, we would expect that the palatalization rule in (15) should apply to the form in (14) because the structural requirements to trigger (15) are met. This is not the case though. This points out a fundamental difference between Malay and Akan, one which can not be predicted by the nature of the rules or representations. We must therefore say that this difference in operation is an option provided by universal grammar to rules, and we will call this the Uniformity Parameter.

The difference between the behavior of the nasal spread rule in Malay and the palatalization rule in Akan then follows from the setting of the Uniformity Parameter in the structural description of the rule. The Uniformity Parameter determines whether a rule requires all environments that a segment appears in to satisfy the structural description of the rule or if only a single environment is sufficient to trigger the rule. All rules will have this parameter set to either *on* which requires all environments be uniform to trigger the rule or *off* which only requires a single instance of a triggering environment to be present.

The nasal spread rule in Malay has its Uniformity Parameter set to *off* which indicates that uniformity of environments is not required to trigger this rule. The *off* setting of the Uniformity Parameter coincides with the overapplication of a rule in a reduplicated form.

The *on* setting for the Uniformity Parameter requires that all environments that a segment appears in satisfy the structural description of a rule in order for that rule to apply. This is the case for the palatalization rule in Akan. By setting the Uniformity Parameter for this rule to *on*, the rule will not apply to the representation in (14) because the segment that undergoes palatalization does not reside in environments that uniformly satisfy the structural description of the palatalization rule.

The /k/ in (14) is in an environment that triggers the palatalization rule [k → ɪ] and at the same time in an environment that does not [k → a]. This situation does not satisfy the Uniformity Parameter setting on the palatalization rule so the rule does not apply.

The most persuasive evidence for the *on* setting of the Uniformity Parameter for the palatalization rule is provided by the reduplicated forms in Akan that do show palatalization. These forms are presented in (16).

(16) a. dʑɪ-dʑe   *gɪ-ge   'receive'
      b. tɕɥi-tɕɥeʔ   *kwi-kwe 'cut'

The [dorsal] segments in these forms occur in *accidentally uniform environments* and are immediately accounted for by the present analysis. Consider the representations in (17).

(17) a. # → g ⇉ e → %
                ɪ

     b. # → k → w → e → ʔ → %
               i

Both of the forms in (17) undergo the palatalization rule and if we consider all the environments the [dorsal] segments appear in we immediately understand why. In (17a) the /g/ appears in two distinct environments, [g → e] and [g → ɪ]. Both of these environments trigger palatalization because in each a [dorsal] segment precedes a non-low non-back vowel.[7] Since both environments trigger the palatalization rule, the Uniformity Parameter for this rule is satisfied and the rule is triggered. (17b) is a similar case with the only modification being that the palatalization rule must be allowed to iterate through the whole onset. Thus, first the /w/ is palatalized since it occurs in a uniform environment that triggers palatalization and after this the /k/ is palatalized from the /w/.

The fact that setting the Uniformity Parameter to *on* correctly predicts the behavior of palatalization in reduplicative forms in Akan is a remarkable finding that lends strong support to this hypothesis. Akan provides support for the Uniformity Parameter not only due to its contrast with Malay in that Akan shows underapplication effects but most importantly, the prediction made by requiring uniformity of the triggering environment is completely confirmed by the forms in (16).

To summarize, the discussion of palatalization in Akan has presented two important points. First, underapplication is due to the Uniformity Parameter. Second, Akan confirms the Uniformity Parameter on the palatalization rule because forms that accidentally satisfy the uniformity requirement on the triggering environment of this rule do show palatalization.

The analysis of backcopying in Raimy (2000) is a major advance over all previous analyses because of the lack of reduplication specific mechanisms. The type of phonological identity that is present in this analysis is the minimal possible kind that is present in all models of phonology. A segment is identical only to itself. This a characteristic of phonology in general.

The assumption of a derivation is also not reduplication specific. Evidence for a derivation in phonology comes primarily from phenomena other than reduplication. In fact reduplication is supposed to be a prime argument against the derivation in phonology according to McCarthy and Prince (1995). Ironically, in the model here derivation is crucial to understanding backcopying effects.

Prelinearization representations and postlinearization representation differ only in how precedence information is represented. Reduplicated forms are phonological representations containing non-asymmetric precedence structure before linearization occurs. Non-asymmetry in a phonological representation causes some segments to occur in multiple environments. Linearization removes non-asymmetrical characteristics from phonological representations by repeating the section of a phonological string that is non-asymmetrical. The repetition that results from linearization splits multiple environments in which a segment appears into simple but distinct environments.

A derivation explains the difference between prelinearization and postlinearization representations as just the application of a process. As long as a process does not apply vacuously, we expect representations to change in the course of a derivation. That representations change over the course of a derivation is the explanation of opacity effects and this was Chomsky's the primary motivation for generative phonology (Chomsky 1975:25-26). Opacity occurs when an environment that is pertinent to the application of a rule is modified after the rule applies. The resulting effect is that it appears that there is an exception to a rule, either a rule applied in a place where it should not have or it didn't apply in a place where it should.

The present analysis of backcopying reduces overapplication and underapplication effects in reduplication to opacity effects. This point refutes the whole typology of overapplication, underapplication and normal application (Wilbur 1973) because the rules that show these characteristics always apply (or fail to apply) in a normal fashion within the context of a derivation. The phenomena of overapplication and underapplication are simple opacity effects resulting from the linearization process affecting phonological representations that are non-asymmetrical in nature. The interaction of phonological rules and reduplication is just a quirk of the complex phonological structures built by reduplicative morphology.

Now that the basic features of the analysis of reduplication have been presented we can turn to other case studies. Each of the following languages has a reduplication pattern that supports the basic claim that no reduplication specific machinery is present nor is any required in the model of reduplication presented here.

2.2.2 *Chumash /l/ deletion*

Chumash (Ineseño) is another case where a phonological process changes its behavior depending on what phonological environments are present. Applegate (1976:281) reports a process that deletes /l/ before dentals ({t, c, s, n, l} for this dialect of Chumash) that underapplies in some reduplicated environments and overapplies in others. Applegate (1976:281) presents the data in (18) to show the underapplication of this process in some reduplicated forms.

(18) s-talik + R   > s-tal-talik   'his wives...'
      c'aluqay + R   > c'al-c'aluqay   'cradles'
      s-pil-kowon + R > s-pil-pilkowon   'it is spilling'

The interesting aspect of this Chumash data is the fact that the /l/ deletion process can overapply in some reduplicative forms. Applegate (1976) only presents one form (in 19) but there is a difference between this form and the forms in (18) that allows the behavior of the of /l/ deletion process to be predicted and understood.

(19) s-pil-tap > spitap +R > s-pit-pitap   'it is falling in'

The form in (19) is a case of overapplication according to McCarthy and Prince (1995:346) because a potential surface form for (19) is the form, *s-pil-pitap*, that shows normal application of the /l/ deletion process is expected given the morphological structure for (19) that they assume. The morphological structure for the form in (19) is as in (20).

(20)

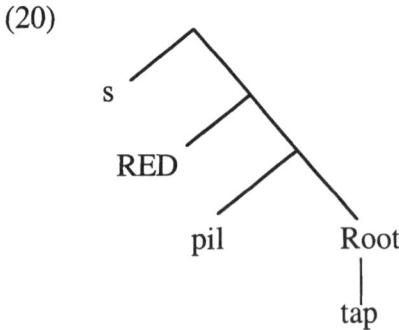

The analysis that is available given the representational advances of the present proposal claims that the behavior of the /l/ deletion rule is dependent on the Derived Environment Condition (Kiparsky 1982). First, we must refine the Derived Environment Condition to only consider segmental material and to ignore precedence information in determining whether a derived environment has been created. In other words, for a Derived Environment Condition on a rule to be satisfied, there must be a precedence relation between segments belonging to two distinct morphemes. In cases where a precedence relation is between two segments of a single morpheme the Derived Environment Condition is not met. Whether a precedence link connects segmental material from a single morpheme or not is an important issue in reduplicated forms. Consider the graph for a form in (18) created by the morphology, shown in (21).

(21) $\# \rightarrow c' \rightarrow a \rightarrow l \rightarrow u \rightarrow q \rightarrow a \rightarrow y \rightarrow \%$

The dotted back link in (21) that creates the loop in this form is the result of a different morpheme from the base. This conceivably could be enough to cause the Derived Environment Condition to be satisfied but it does not for this example. The reason for this is that although the dotted back link has been added to the base, this precedence link connects segments from a single morpheme. Throughout this chapter we will find that this sort of reduplication does not count as a derived environment. Chapter 3 will claim that many reduplication patterns (if not all) result from readjustment rules and that readjustment rules in general do not count as derived environments. Returning to (21), the segmental material of two morphemes do not become adjacent as a result of the reduplicative morpheme and consequently the Derived Environment Condition is not met.

   The Derived Environment Condition is met in the form in (19) because the /l/ that eventually deletes is from a different morpheme from the coronal that follows it. How the Derived Environment Condition is met in this graph is readily apparent if the different morphemes are distinguished graphically as in (22). The order of affixation is directly derived from the morphological tree in (20) and each morpheme is presented on a separate row.

(22) a. $\# \rightarrow t \rightarrow a \rightarrow p \rightarrow \%$ b. $\# \rightarrow t \rightarrow a \rightarrow p \rightarrow \%$
$$p \rightarrow i \rightarrow l$$

c. $\# \rightarrow t \rightarrow a \rightarrow p \rightarrow \%$ d. $\# \rightarrow t \Rightarrow a \rightarrow p \rightarrow \%$
$$p \rightarrow i \rightarrow l \qquad\qquad p \rightarrow i \rightarrow l$$
$$s$$

(22a) shows the root itself before any affixation occurs. (22b) shows the concatenation of /pil/ which is a prefix. (22c) then shows the concatenation of the loop triggered by the reduplicative morpheme. Finally, (22d) shows the final affixation of the prefix /s/.

The complex graph of segmental material that is built by the morphology module contains all of the information that is needed for the /l/ deletion rule to apply in (21) but not in (22d). The crucial aspect of the representation in (22d) is that the /l/ deletion rule is not triggered by the phonological material added as the spell out of the reduplicated morpheme. This material is indicated by the dashed back link from /l/ to /p/. As in (21) this link connects the segmental material from a single morpheme to itself and thus does not satisfy the Derived Environment Condition. Instead, the Derived Environment Condition on the /l/ deletion rule is satisfied by the precedence link from /l/ to /t/ (added as part of the prefixation of /pil/ in [22b]) that *does* link segmental material from two distinct morphemes.

The difference in morphological composition between the forms in (21) and (22d) allows the behavior of the /l/ deletion rule in Chumash to be predicted but this is only one relevant aspect of this particular set of data. The nature of the /l/ deletion rule itself must now be investigated.

Deletion processes raise interesting questions about how these processes affect a precedence structure. There are three basic possible interpretations of deletion of an entire segment in a precedence structure. The first possibility is to actually remove the deleted segment. The problem with this approach to deletion given the present representations is that removing a segment creates a break in the precedence structure which must then be repaired. Because of the additional requirement of making a repair to the resulting precedence structure, this first interpretation of deletion will be set aside as we consider other alternatives.

A different interpretation of deletion is to combine the "deleted" segment with another one. This operation would coalesce two segments and the precedence information regarding these segments into a single segment. Deletion as coalescence will be symbolized by putting a dashed circle around a description of the segments that should be affected. /l/ "deletion" in Chumash can be represented as in (23).

(23)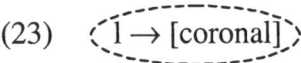

(23) indicates that a sequence of /l/ followed by a coronal should be combined into a single segment. Coalescence as a process removes the precedence structure that occurs between the segments that are combined. Applying (23) to the representation in (22d) produces the precedence graph in (24b). (24a) indicates the segments that are affected by (23) by putting a dotted circle around them and (24b) shows the result of the coalescence of these segments.

(24)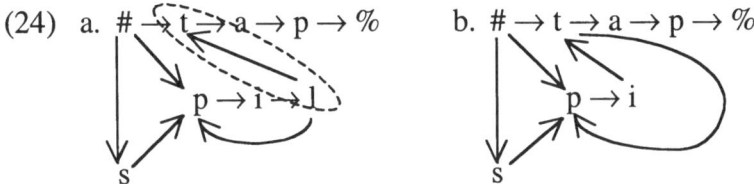

Linearizing (24b) produces the correct output form and this shows that a coalescence approach to deletion is available in Chumash.

An alternative to the coalescence analysis of deletion is one where a precedence link is added to "jump over" the deleted segment. This approach to /l/ deletion in Chumash would posit a rule that adds a precedence link from the segment preceding /l/ to the segment that follows /l/. Explicit formulation of this kind of rule will be addressed in chapter 3 so for now only the result of this particular rule will be shown. Adding a jumping link over /l/ as an approach to deletion would produce the precedence graph in (25) from (22d). The added jump link is indicated by a dotted arrow.

(25)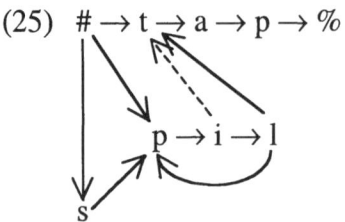

Although the jump approach to deletion is a plausible analysis for /l/ deletion in Chumash it does not produce the correct results. There is no possible linearization of the graph in (25) that produces the correct form *spitpitap*. Linearization will begin with the sequence of *#spi* and then be faced with the decision to follow the added jump link or not. If the jump link is followed then the resulting linearized form is **#spitap%* with no /l/ or reduplication because the beginning of the loop is anchored on the skipped /l/ segment. The alternative linearization is to ignore the jump link at first and follow it after the reduplicative loop has been used but this produces **#spilpitap%* (an outcome that shows "normal application" of the /l/ deletion rule) which is also incorrect. Because of this result, the coalescence approach to /l/ deletion will be adopted for Chumash: it should be noted here that in chapter 3 the jump link analysis of deletion will be crucial in accounting for reduplication in Tohono O'odham and both the coalescence and jump link interpretation of deletion are required to account for Indonesian.

To summarize the present case study of the interaction of Chumash /l/ deletion and reduplication, an analysis of over and under application of /l/ deletion in Chumash based on the proposals in this chapter has been presented. /l/ deletion is reanalyzed as the coalescence of /l/ with a following coronal segment. This coalescence rule requires the Derived Environment Condition to be met. Cases where "/l/ deletion" appears to overapply are ones that satisfy the Derived Environment Condition and cases where "/l/ deletion" appears to underapply do not. The surface appearance of over- and underapplication is an opacity effect that results from the linearization process eliminating parts of the whole precedence graph.

It must be restated that this analysis accounts for the intricate interaction between reduplication and /l/ deletion without any recourse to any type of surface evaluated Identity Constraint (Wilbur 1973) or correspondence (McCarthy and Prince 1995). Instead, this is another case that shows that the simple ordering of processes in a derivational model of phonology can empirically and conceptually account for reduplication and associated phenomena.

2.2.3 Chaha /x/ dissimilation

Kenstowicz and Banksira (1999) analyze Chaha as providing another case of backcopying. The process in question is continuant dissimilation that derives [k] from /x/ when /x/ is followed by a [+cont, -son] segment. Banksira (1997) argues that [k] is a derived segment, coming from either a dissimilated /x/ or from the simplification of a geminate /x/. It is the presence of [k] in reduplicated forms that is at issue here. A sampling of the data Kenstowicz and Banksira (1999) present that represents the distribution of [k] and [x] is found in (26) and (27). Note that the original source of the data is Banksira (1997). All forms are presented in the 3rd person masculine singular.

(26) a. /x/ in final position of radical

Jussive	Imperfect	Perfect	Gloss	Root
yə-frɨx	yɨ-fərx	fənəx[8]	'tolerate'	/frx/
yə-məs(ɨ)x	yɨ-mes(ɨ)x	mesəx	'chew'	/msx/
yə-t-ʃaməx	yɨ-t-ʃaməx	tə-ʃaməx	'lean on'	/symx/

b. /x/ in initial position of radical

Jussive	Gloss	Root
y-a-xətɨr	'precede'	/xtr/
yə-xrəm	'spend year'	/xrm/
yə-xʷərɨr	'amputate'	/xwr/

Now compare the following forms, also in 3rd singular masculine Jussive, that contain /x/ in the initial position of the radical but have a [+cont, -son] segment (/f, s, z, ʕ/) following in the radical.

(27) | *Jussive* | *Gloss* | *Root* |
|---|---|---|
| yə-kzəβ | 'become inferior' | /xzβ/ |
| yə-kad | 'deny' | /xʕd/^{9} |
| yə-kfɨr | 'separate' | /xfr/ |
| yə-kəsɨs | 'accuse' | /xs/ |
| yə-ktɨf | 'hash' | /xtf/ |

(26a) shows that underlying /x/ is realized as [x] when it is in final position in a root. (26b) presents cases where /x/ is in initial position of the root and appears as [x] because it is not followed by a [+cont, -son] segment. (27) presents cases where /x/ is realized as [k] because a [+cont, -son] segment follows. The form *yə-ktɨf* 'hash' is particularly interesting because it shows that the dissimilation of /x/ due to a following [+cont, -son] segment does not appear to be a strictly local operation. We will ignore this aspect of the dissimilation process of /x/ and assume the rule in (28) adequately characterizes this process.

(28) /x/ → [-cont]   / _...[+cont, -son]

This is the level of formulation of this process (translating Kenstowicz and Banksira's constraint into a rule) offered by Kenstowicz and Banksira (1999) so the analysis being developed here can be equated with that offered by Kenstowicz and Banksira on this point. This is important if we are to compare the analysis presented here against the one presented by Kenstowicz and Banksira.

Given the rule in (28) and the representations already presented in earlier sections, we can account for the backcopying phenomena in reduplicative forms. Kenstowicz and Banksira (1999:578, 580) present the following examples of total reduplication and final reduplication.

(29) a. Total reduplication with a [+cont, -son] in the root

kəskɨs		'smash'	/xs/
kaka		'dry totally'	/xʕ/
kyəkyɨf	< /kyəfkyɨf/	'sprinkle'	/xyf/

b. Total reduplication without [+cont, -son] in the root

kətkɨt		'crush'	/xt/
a-ŋ-kʷətkʷɨt		'remove weeds'	/xwt/
kəkɨm	< /kəmkɨm/	'trim'	/xm/
a-ŋ-kʷərkʷɨr		'make lump'	/xwr/
kəkɨr	< /kərkɨr/	'hold in armpit'	/xr/

c. Final reduplication

sɨkɨk		'drive a peg'	/sx/
a-fʷkɨk		'squat'	/fwx/
əkɨk		'scratch'	/ʕx/
bʷəkək		'talk a lot'	/bwx/

Kenstowicz and Banksira echo McCarthy and Prince's claim that a derivational approach to reduplication can not account for the back-copying effects present in (29b). Backcopying is present in the forms in (29b) because it is the /x/ itself that is causing /x/ to dissimilate to [k]. This must be the case because there are no other [+cont, -son] segments in the root to trigger the /x/ dissimilation. Backcopying is also present in (29c) because /x/ is in final position of the root and thus no triggering segment could follow. This effect is accounted for in a natural way within the present proposals though. Consider the representation in (30).

(30) /xt/   kətkɨt   'crush'

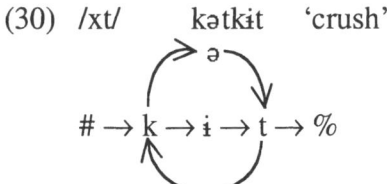

Given this phonological representation, two issues must be addressed. The first one is how the non-concatenative nature of Semitic phonology is affected by the proposals on the representation of reduplication made here. The second will be how the long distance character of this continuant dissimilation process can be encoded in these new representations.

The main impact that the proposals here have on Semitic morphology is to bring non-concatenative morphology much closer in nature to concatenative morphology than previously thought. This situation is created by the ability for the morphological component to directly alter overall precedence structures in underlying representations by simply adding new precedence relationships. The well recognized difference between concatenative and non-concatenative morphology can be reduced to a difference in the precedence relationships added by affixes. Concatenative morphology in general only contains precedence relations in affixes that produce prefixes or suffixes while non-concatenative morphology instantiates more affixes that have infix like precedence relations.[10]

For the purposes of the present examples, we can assume that the morphological component produces the phonological representation in (30). The crucial aspect of (30) that is relevant to the present discussion is the looping structure that indicates there will be repetition of the consonants. Whether (30) is monomorphemic and thus stored as it is represented or polymorphemic and constructed within the morphology is orthogonal to the analysis of /x/ dissimilation that will be developed here. Consequently this issue will be left aside so we can focus on more pertinent ones.

Given a representation like (30), the long distance character of the /x/ dissimilation process that derives [k] from /x/ can be understood as a search in the precedence graph for a [+cont, -son] segment. Apparently, this process is triggered by the presence of /x/ in an underlying form.[11] To find the answer to this question, a search that follows the precedence relations is begun from any /x/. This search is iterative in that the precedence graph is followed until either a [+cont, -son] segment is found or the end of the precedence structure is reached. With this understanding we can return to (30).

The reduplicated form in (30) shows the alternation of /x/ to [k] because the loop in this representation allows the continuant search to find the segment that initiated this search. Forms that have a surface [x] are all forms that do not show reduplication (and thus do not have a loop) and do not have a continuant segment following the /x/ either locally or at a distance. This difference is shown in (31).

(31) a. yə-xdɨr   /xdr/   'thatch'

$$\# \to x \to d \to \dot{\imath} \to r \to \%$$
$$y \to ə$$

b. yə-kfɨr   /xfr/   'separate'

$$\# \to x \to f \to \dot{\imath} \to r \to \% \qquad \Rightarrow \qquad \# \to k \to f \to \dot{\imath} \to r \to \%$$
$$y \to ə \qquad\qquad\qquad\qquad\qquad y \to ə$$

c. kətkɨt   /xt/   'crush'

$$\# \to x \to \dot{\imath} \to t \to \% \qquad \Rightarrow \qquad \# \to k \to \dot{\imath} \to t \to \%$$

If we consider the paths that can be followed starting from the /x/ in each of the forms in (31), we can see why dissimilation occurs in (31b,c) but not (31a). In (31a), if we follow a precedence path starting from /x/ we reach the end of the graph before any [+cont, -son] segment is reached. Thus, no dissimilation. (31b) is a very similar situation except that a [+cont, -son] segment is found before the end of the graph is reached and this triggers the /x/ dissimilation rule. The reduplicated form in (31c) also shows a successful search for a [+cont, -son] segment, thus triggering dissimilation. The crucial part of (31c) is the precedence link from /x/ to /t/. This is what creates the loop that allows the /x/ to find itself and thus trigger dissimilation.

This analysis accounts for the total reduplication and final reduplication facts presented by Kenstowicz and Banksira (1999). The backcopying effect seen in these types of reduplication is due to the /x/ segment "finding itself" via the loop in the phonological representation and thus triggering dissimilation. Later in the derivation, linearization occurs and produces the surface form that shows overapplication and backcopying of the /x/ dissimilation process.

Continuing the analysis of backcopying in Chaha, there is an interesting twist when cases of medial reduplication are considered. Consider the forms in (32) which add new facts to the overall pattern of /x/ dissimilation.

(32)   a. [+cont, -son] roots
       Nonfrequentive

Imperative	Imperfect	Perfect	Gloss	Root
nɨk(ɨ)s	yɨ-rək(ɨ)s	nəkəs	'bite'	/rxs/
nɨk(ɨ)f	yɨ-rək(ɨ)f	nəkəf	'quarrel'	/rxf/
fɨka	yɨ-fəka	fəka	'flee'	/fxʕ/

Frequentive

Imperative	Imperfect	Perfect	Gloss	Root
tɨkək(ɨ)s	yɨ-tkək(ɨ)s	tɨkəkəs	'burn'	/txs/
tə-rkakəf	yɨ-tɨ-rkakəf	tə-rkakəf	'quarrel'	/rxf/
a-fkaka	y-a-fkaka	a-fkaka	'vanish'	/fxʕ/

       b. no [+cont, -son] roots
       Nonfrequentive

Imperative	Imperfect	Perfect	Gloss	Root
sɨxər	yɨ-sxər	səkər	'get drunk'	/sxr/
mɨxɨr	yɨ-məxɨr	məkər	'advise'	/mxr/
nɨxəβ	yɨ-rəkɨβ	nəkəβ	'find'	/rxβ/

Frequentive

Imperative	Imperfect	Perfect	Gloss	Root
tə-sxaxər	yɨ-t-sɨkakər	tə-skakər	'act naughtily'	/sxr/
tə-mxaxər	yɨ-tɨ-mkakər	tə-mkakər	'advise e. o.'	/mxr/
tə-rxəxəβ [12]	yɨ-tɨ-rkəkəβ	tə-rkəkəβ	'show up'	/rxβ/

The important aspect of the forms in (32) is that there is no dissimilation of /x/ to [k] in the frequentive imperative forms in (32b) while dissimilation of /x/ is present in all other frequentive forms. Another related issue is to explain the presence of [k] in the nonfrequentive perfect forms in (32b). These [k]s appear to be unconditioned. These two anomalies must be accounted for in some manner.

The anomalies are resolved once we consider the morphology that distinguishes the forms in (32). Specifically, we must take note of a gemination process that is triggered in the imperfective and perfective forms (but not the imperative) by the addition of the /-t(ə)-/ morpheme to the frequentive forms in (32) (Banksira 1997, Kenstowicz and Banksira 1999). Awareness of this process allows us to understand the unique behavior of the imperative frequentive forms in the following way. Note that there is a general degemination process active in Chaha (Banksira 1997:76) which will undo the morphological gemination at a point later in the derivation.

The analysis presented here will show that the reason why the imperative frequentive forms in (32b) do not have a surface [k] is that the continuant dissimilation process only applies in *nonderived environments*. As in the analysis of Chumash, whether added phonological material qualifies as a derived environment is dependent on whether segmental material from one morpheme is connected to segmental material from another morpheme. Chaha will provide strong evidence that added precedence structures that do not contain segmental material and only connect segments from a single morpheme do not count as derived environments.

The morphology of Semitic languages is complex with importance given to both roots and templates (McCarthy 1979). This view of Semitic morphology causes all representations given to the phonology by the morphology to be morphologically complex. Determining what parts of these morphologically complex forms count as derived environments and which parts do not allows the application of the /x/ dissimilation process in Chaha to be understood.

From the cases of total and final reduplication in Chaha already analyzed it appears that however a template is interpreted its combination with a root does not count as a derived environment. Consider the representations in (33) examples of final and total reduplication are presented.

(33) a. # → s → i → x → %   ⇒   # → s → i → k → %

b.

→ x → i → t → %   ⇒   # → k → i → t → %

Both final reduplication and total reduplication result from templatic pressure requiring a final consonant. This forces the looping structure in both (33a) and (33b). Both representations in (33) show the application of /x/ dissimilation so all of the precedence relationships attributed to a template do not count as derived environments. Additional morphemes added to the root and template structure do act as derived environments though.

Cases of total and final reduplication in Chaha can now be contrasted with the frequentive forms of verbs presented in (32). These forms have the middle consonant of the root reduplicated in response to being in the frequentive. This can be seen when the nonfrequentive forms are considered. By restricting the /x/ dissimilation rule to applying only in nonderived environments, only certain parts of the precedence structure in frequentive imperative are relevant in determining whether /x/ dissimilation should apply. Consider the frequentive imperative forms again, below as (34), along with representative graph representations.

(34) a. /x/ followed by a [+cont, -son] roots
        nɨkək(ɨ)s   'bite'   /rxs/
        tɨkək(ɨ)s   'burn'   /txs/
        tə-rkakəf   'quarrel'   /rxf/
        a-fkaka   'vanish'   /fxʕ/

      b. tə-rkakəf   'quarrel'   /rxf/

$$\# \rightarrow r \rightarrow x \Rightarrow \mathfrak{o} \rightarrow f \; \rangle \; \% \Rightarrow \quad \# \rightarrow r \rightarrow k \Rightarrow \mathfrak{o} \rightarrow f \rightarrow \%$$

$$t \rightarrow \mathfrak{o} \quad a \qquad\qquad t \rightarrow \mathfrak{o} \quad a$$

c. /x/ not followed by a [+cont, -son] roots

tə-sxaxər	'act naughtily'	/sxr/
tə-mxaxər	'advise each other'	/mxr/
tə-rxəxəβ	'show up'	/rxβ/

d. tə-sxaxər   'act naughtily'   /sxr/

$$\# \rightarrow s \rightarrow x \Rightarrow \mathfrak{o} \rightarrow r \rightarrow \%$$

$$t \rightarrow \mathfrak{o} \quad a$$

The different behaviors of the forms in (34a) and (34c) are directly accounted for by the claim that /x/ dissimilation only occurs in non-derived environments. This claim limits the search function of the /x/ dissimilation rule to only certain parts of the precedence structures in (34b) and (34d). Precedence relations that count as derived environments are indicated by dashed arrow lines. Crucially, these paths can be attributed to an infixed /a/[13] that anchors its preceding and following links on the middle consonant of the root. The spell-out of the frequentive morpheme in Chaha is this infixed looping vowel. The reduplicating loop of the infixed vowel counts as a derived environment because of the segmental material associated with it. Following from this point, these paths will be ignored by the /x/ dissimilation rule. The forms in (34a) show application of the /x/ dissimilation process because of the [+cont, -son] segment that follows the /x/ in the root, not because of the loop in the phonological representation added by the frequentive morpheme. The forms in (34c) do not show /x/ dissimilation because there are no [+cont, -son] segments that follow the /x/ if links and segments that are derived environments are ignored.

The forms that must still be accounted for in (32) are the perfective and imperfective forms of frequentive and nonfrequentive verbs in (32b). As before, once we investigate the morphology in-

volved in these forms, we will see that they follow the same generalizations and principles as all other forms. There are no exceptions.

Abstracting away from some vowel changes, one of the differences between the frequentive and nonfrequentive forms is the
presence of the reflexive-passive morpheme /-t(ə)-/.[14] One reflex of
this morpheme is the gemination of the middle radical in the imperfect and perfect forms but *not* the imperative forms. Morphologically triggered gemination is the key to understanding the nature of
the /x/ dissimilation present in the remaining data in (32). A representative sample of these remaining forms is presented in (35).

(35)   Nonfrequentive

Imperfect	Perfect	Gloss	Root
yɨ-sxər	səkər	'get drunk'	/sxr/
yɨ-məxər	məkər	'advise'	/mxr/
yɨ-rəxɨβ	nəkəβ	'find'	/rxβ/

Frequentive

Imperfect	Perfect	Gloss	Root
yɨ-t-sɨkakər	tə-skakər	'act naughtily'	/sxr/
yɨ-tɨ-mkakər	tə-mkakər	'advise each other'	/mxr/
yɨ-tɨ-rkəkəβ	tə-rkəkəβ	'show up'	/rxβ/

Where morphological gemination occurs will explain the pattern of
/x/ dissimilation in all of the forms in (35).

All of the frequentive forms undergo gemination of the second
radical as the result of the presence of the /t(ə)/ morpheme (Banksira 1997). Morphological gemination in Chaha will be accounted
for through the addition of a precedence relation from the medial
consonant of a triliteral radical back to itself. Since the addition of
this particular link does not add any segmental material it will not
be a derived environment (just as in the Chumash /l/ deletion example in section 2.2.2) and thus can trigger /x/ dissimilation. With this
view of morphological gemination in mind, consider the representations for the frequentive imperfect in (36) where derived environments are indicated by dashed arrows.

(36) a. yɨ-t-sɨkakər   'act naughtily'   /sxr/

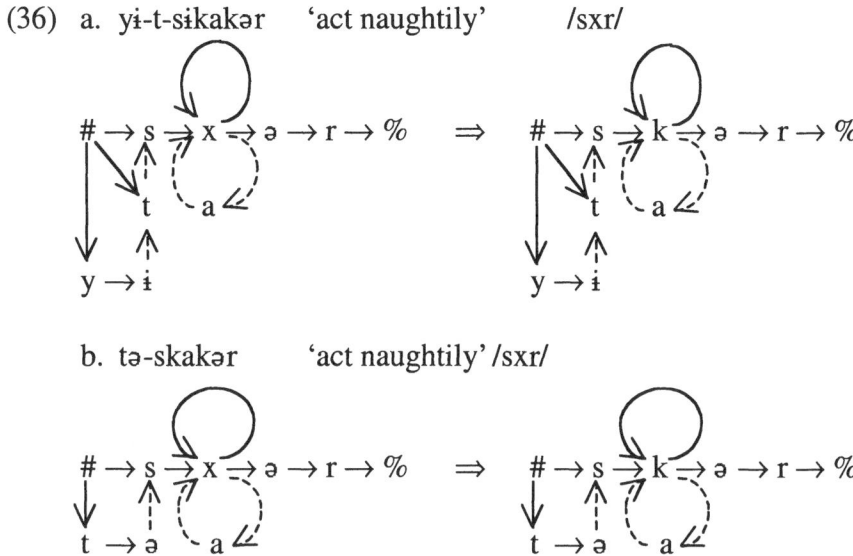

   b. tə-skakər   'act naughtily' /sxr/

The gemination of the middle consonant of the radical caused by
the frequentive morpheme /-tə-/ is indicated by the self loop in the
imperfect form in (36a) and in the perfect form in (36b). This self
loop is the source of the application of the /x/ dissimilation rule
since it counts as a nonderived environment because it links a segment back onto itself without adding any segmental material. Since
no segmental material is present in this gemination rule, the added
precedence link counts as a nonderived environment. Given this
aspect of frequentive morphology, /x/ dissimilation acts in a completely normal way in these forms. The gemination does not appear
in the surface form because of a later degemination process.

   Gemination of the second radical is also part of the marking of
perfective forms (Banksira 1997). Consequently the nonfrequentive
imperfect forms in (35) do not show the effects of the /x/ dissimilation because there is no morphological gemination or [+cont, -son]
segment to trigger the process. The nonfrequentive perfect forms
are analogous to the frequentive forms in (35-36) because perfect
morphology also triggers gemination of the middle consonant of the
root. The representational difference between the nonfrequentive
imperfect and perfect forms resulting from morphological gemination is presented in (37).

(37) a. yɨ-sxər   'get drunk' /sxr/

$$\# \to \underset{\overset{\big\uparrow}{y \to ɨ}}{\underset{}{s}} \to x \to ə \to r \to \%$$

b. səkər   'get drunk' /sxr/

$$\# \to s \to ə \to x \to ə \to \% \Rightarrow \quad \# \to s \to ə \to k \to ə \to \%$$

(37a) shows the nonfrequentive imperfect form that does not undergo morphological gemination. Without morphological gemination, whether /x/ dissimilation occurs or not is derived from whether
there is a following [+cont, -son] segment in the representation.
(37b) shows the nonfrequentive perfect form with morphological
gemination. The looping structure of the geminate allows the /x/ to
find itself and trigger the /x/ dissimilation process.

   This completes the analysis of the interaction of reduplication
and /x/ dissimilation in Chaha. The most important aspect of this
analysis is that the complex surface facts are accounted for through
the principled interaction of morphological and phonological processes. Once the phonological structures that spell-out particular
morphemes are identified, the application of /x/ dissimilation behaves in a completely normal way but only in nonderived environments. This finding argues against the Kenstowicz and Banksira
(1999) claim that Chaha presents evidence in favor of correspondence theory (McCarthy and Prince 1995). In fact, the argument
that Chaha provides evidence for output-output correspondence
made by Kenstowicz and Banksira can be used as an argument in
favor of the analysis presented here.

   The approach to Chaha reduplication presented here is superior
to the analysis presented by Kenstowicz and Banksira (1999) because there is no exceptional behavior required of the /x/ dissimilation process in any of the forms in the proposed rule based analysis.
In contrast, Kenstowicz and Banksira crucially require an extra output-output correspondence in order to account for the frequentive

imperative forms. Since this output-output correspondence is limited only to the frequentive imperative forms and is not motivated by anything but the /x/ dissimilation facts, it is equivalent to marking these forms as exceptional using an ad hoc notation when compared to an analysis that does not single out these morphological form. An analysis that does not have to single out a group of forms as being exceptional and undergoing an additional process is superior to an analysis that does. Analyses that account for a language with general processes that are not limited to certain classes of forms present a deeper understanding of the language as a whole when compared with analyses that require additional mechanisms. The rule based analysis presented here is thus superior to the Optimality Theory based analysis presented by Kenstowicz and Banksira (1999) because it provides a deeper insight into how the morphology and phonology of Chaha is organized. Since this rule based analysis is superior to the Optimality Theory account we can conclude that contra Kenstowicz and Banksira (1999), Chaha does not provide any evidence in favor of correspondence theory (McCarthy and Prince 1995) or Optimality Theory (Prince and Smolensky 1993) at all. Instead, Chaha presents a case where a modular rule based analysis of reduplication utilizing the representations proposed here provides an analysis that reveals a well behaved, although complex, morphological and phonological system. Additionally, Chaha provides more evidence that loops that do not contain segmental material are not derived environments.

2.2.4 Southern Paiute

McCarthy and Prince (1995) present Southern Paiute as another example of a language with underapplication effects. The particular process in Southern Paiute that underapplies is a nasalization of /w/ to [ŋʷ]. Sapir (1930) claims that all instances of [ŋʷ] are derived either from /w/ or /m/ through either the /w/ nasalization process or the spirantization of /m/. The nasalization of /w/ occurs between vowels in derived environments. Complicating this distribution of /w/ is another separate process that inserts [w] between a preceding

/u/ and a following vowel (Sapir 1930: 57). These processes nasal-izing /w/ and inserting [w] to break up vowel hiatus create an intri-cate distribution of where [ŋʷ] and [w] surface that does not appear to interact with reduplication. We will begin the investigation of the interaction between /w/ nasalization and reduplication by reviewing Sapir's statements on the realization of /w/.

The basic generalization for the /w/ nasalization process that Sapir presents is that word initial /w/ appears as [ŋʷ] when it comes to follow a vowel due to derivation or compounding (Sapir 1930: 49). Sapir presents the following forms to support this generaliza-tion. Note that the forms in (38) have been updated to reflect IPA transcription according to *The Handbook of the International Pho-netic Alphabet* (1999) with IPA palatal segments, /ç, ʝ/, representing what Sapir calls "anterior palatal spirants" and velar fricatives /ɣ, x/ representing "back palatal spirants" segments (Sapir 1930:45).

(38)   waʔaɲi-   tɯː-ŋʷaʔaɲi-   'to shout/to give a good shout'

wɯ̈nɪ-   yaŋʷɪ-ŋʷɯ̈nɪ-jaʔ   'to stand/while standing and holding'

waija-   nɪaːβɪ-ŋʷaija-pːɪ̯   'to have council/council of chiefs'

w̥a̰ʔtʃɯ-   ʃu(w)a-ŋ̊ʷa̰ʔtjɯpːɯɣaʔ   'to catch up with/nearly caught up with'

w(ʔ)itsɯʔ-   tɯʔra-ŋʔʷɪntsiʔɪtsː   'bird/horned lark (lit. desert bird)'

Sapir (1930:49-50) points out that this nasalization process does not apply to /w/ when it follows a vowel due to reduplication. Redupli-cation in these forms consists of prefixing a CV reduplicant.

(39)   wɯɣɯ-   'vulva'   wɯwɯxɯa̰   'vulvas (obj.)'

wayi-   'several enter'   wawaxːɪ̯pɯɣaʔ   'all entered'

wɯnːai-   'to throw'   wɯwɯnʔnai-   'several throw down'

waʔatʃɪɣɪ-   'to whoop'   waʔwaʔᵃtʃɪɣɪ   'to whoop sev-eral times'

The difference between the two behaviors seen in (38) and (39) can be characterized by simply placing a Derived Environment Condition on the /w/ nasalization process. Given this approach, the environment that triggers the /w/ nasalization process must be composed of segmental material from two separate morphemes. The view that this /w/ nasalization process only operates in derived environments is supported by Sapir's own statement that, "When an initial *w* comes, *by derivation or compounding*, to stand after a vowel, it regularly becomes nasalized to -ŋw-" (Sapir 1930:49) (emphasis mine). Additionally, once this condition is placed on the /w/ nasalization process, the behavior of /w/ in reduplicated forms is predicted by the model of reduplication developed so far.

The requirement that a derived environment must consist of the contact of segmental material from two different morphemes directly accounts for the underapplication affects seen in (39). This data actually just shows the normal nonapplication of the /w/ nasalization process in a nonderived environment. Consider the following examples of application and nonapplication of /w/ nasalization based on whether the Derived Environment Condition is met or not in (40).

(40) a. wũ̃ɪnɪ-   yaŋʷɪ-ŋʷũ̃ɪnɪ-jaʔ
      'to stand'   'while standing and holding'

    b. wɯn:ai-   wɯwɯnʔnai-
       'to throw'   'several throw down'

As in previous examples, the dashed precedence links indicate derived environments thus the compound verb in (40a) shows /w/ nasalization because the Derived Environment Condition is met. The reduplicated form in (40b) does not show the effects of /w/ nasalization because there is no derived environment to trigger the application of the process. The addition of the reduplicative loop does not satisfy the Derived Environment Condition in this case because no segmental material is added along with it. This behavior confirms the same behavior of reduplicated structures in the previous analyses of Chumash and Chaha.

The behavior of the reduplicated forms and nonreduplicated forms in relation to the /w/ nasalization rule has now been accounted for. Other forms that indicate that all /w/s do not nasalize when found between vowels must now be discussed. Sapir (1930:57) states that, "After a primary *u (o)* a *w*, indicated as ^{w} if weak, often slips in before an immediately following vowel." This process introduces [w]s that do not nasalize. Note that since these [w]s are inserted by phonological rule, they should satisfy the Derived Environment Condition and nasalize. Obviously from the data this is not the case and this fact must be explained. Data presented by Sapir (1930:57) to illustrate these [w]s (in bold) is presented in (41).

(41) tua-   tuwatsını̦   'son'/'my son'
      -ɣu-   iβi'-juwʌn̦a̦   'he'/'when he drank'
      puʔɪ   puʔᵂɪ-   'eye'
      -u(w)ɪt:uɣwa-   nɯo(**W**)ɪtux:w̦a̦   'before'/'before me'

These forms can be naturally and easily accounted for in the present derivational analysis by placing the [w] insertion rule in the postcyclic block of rules. By doing this, the insertion of intervocalic [w]s will be after the application of the /w/ nasalization rule, which is cyclic as indicated by its sensitivity to derived environments. Consequently, these inserted [w]s will not be nasalized. Further evidence in support of the late ordering or [w] insertion is Sapir's indication that the actual realization of these inserted [w]s can vary phonetically and thus they appear to be a late, phonetically driven change in the forms.

To complete the analysis of the interaction of /w/ nasalization and reduplication in Southern Paiute, two final points must be addressed. The first point is a clarification of an erroneous form that McCarthy and Prince cite. The second point is an apparent exceptional form.

In their analysis of Southern Paiute, McCarthy and Prince (1995:350, ex 138b) claim that the form *yaŋ*^{w}*ɪ-ŋ*^{w}*ũ̃nɪ-jaʔ* 'while standing and holding' shows a case of normal application of the /w/ nasalization process in a reduplicated form. The representation that they present for this form has the preceding [ŋ^{w}i] corresponding with the following [ŋ^{w}i] which makes the inherent claim that this form is reduplicated in some way. The claim that this form shows reduplication of any form is not supported by either Sapir (1930) or Sapir (1931). Sapir (1931:722) lists *yaŋ*^{w}*ɪ-* as a separate stem that means 'to carry'. This listing, along with the fact that Sapir (1930:49) lists the form in question with forms that do not show reduplication, indicate that *yaŋ*^{w}*ɪ-ŋ*^{w}*ũ̃nɪ-jaʔ* is a compound of some sort and does not have reduplication. Thus, there is no evidence that /w/ nasalization occurs in anything but derived environments as claimed by Sapir and the present analysis.

The final point that must be addressed is the analysis of an exceptional form. The form in question is *a:ɣa-wantʃɯ-* 'to hide'. This form is exceptional on many levels. Most obviously, this form presents an exception to the /w/ nasalization rule applying in derived environments. To compound this complexity, there are other conjugations of this form that have the /w/ nasalized, *a:ɣa-ŋ*^{w}*antʃɪ-ŋqɯ-m*^{w}*ɪʔ* 'has been hiding from' (Sapir 1931:552), and reduplicated forms of this particular construction can have either both /w/s nasalized, *a:ɣa-ŋ*^{w}*aŋ*^{w}*antʃɯ-qai-βaʔ* 'shall have (it) hidden' (Sapir 1931:552), or just the first /w/ nasalized, *a:ja-ŋ*^{w}*aʔwantʃɯ-yɪ-nɪ̥* 'has been hiding me several times' (Sapir 1931:552). This is a very complicated pattern consisting of forms that have multiple different morphemes.

A possible account, admittedly inelegant, for these forms is the following. This analysis is based on the assumption that Sapir is correct in identifying this set of forms as being exceptional and not indicative of some subpattern present in the /w/ nasalization process. The approach will use an ad hoc exception mark (Chomsky and Halle 1968) to indicate not that the whole stem *wantʃɯ-* is exempt from the /w/ nasalization process but instead that certain morphological constructions built on this stem are exempt. Using ideas from Distributed Morphology (Halle and Marantz 1993), this exception feature can be added by a readjustment rule that is triggered by certain morphemes. This approach will immediately allow the forms *a:ɣa-wantʃɯ-* 'to hide', *a:ɣa-ŋʷantʃɪ-ŋqɯ-mʷʔ?* 'has been hiding from', and *a:ɣa-ŋʷaŋʷantʃɯ-qai-βaʔ* 'shall have (it) hidden' to be accounted for. The form *a:ɣa-wantʃɯ-* 'to hide' is accounted for by placing the "no /w/ nasalization" feature on it and the forms *a:ɣa-ŋʷantʃɪ-ŋqɯ-mʷʔ?* 'has been hiding from', and *a:ɣa-ŋʷaŋʷantʃɯ-qai-βaʔ* 'shall have hidden it' are accounted for by not having this feature. Both of these forms show the regular application of /w/ nasalization if we set the /w/ nasalization rule's Uniformity Parameter to *off*. By doing this, the single environment added by the prefixation of *a:ɣa-* to *a:ɣa-ŋʷaŋʷantʃɯ-qai-βaʔ* 'shall have hidden it' is sufficient to trigger /w/ nasalization because it provides not only an intervocalic environment but the crucial derived environment aspect to this form.

At this point, there only remains the form *a:ja-ŋʷaʔwantʃɯ-yɪ-nɪ* 'has been hiding me several times' to be accounted for. This form is extremely troublesome for the following reasons. Due to the lack of identity effects, this form indicates that the morpheme initial [ŋʷ] resulted from a postlinearization process. If this change occurred before linearization, then both underlying /w/s should become [ŋʷ] since they are in actuality the same segment. Continuing with this line of reasoning, a postlinearization /w/ nasalization process does not appear to be a viable option because not all surface [w]s are nasalized. Previously, we accounted for this effect by the late insertion of /w/ to break up /uV/ hiatus and this position prevents us from adding a postlinearization /w/ nasalization process. To completely kill the idea of a tenable post linearization /w/ nasalization process, we must note that even if we ordered the postcyclic /w/ nasalization process before [w] epenthesis to break up certain hiatal constructions, this would not explain why the remaining [w] in *a:ja-ŋʷaʔwantʃɯ-yɪ-nɪ* is not nasalized. Since we are operating in the postcyclic block of phonological rules we can not invoke a Derived Environment Condition.

A viable option available to account for this form is to posit this as a true case of allomorphy. This position is similar to Marantz's (1982) position used to account for certain cases of overapplication. This position would posit *waʔwantʃɯ* as an allomorph of *wantʃɯ* that would only surface in this particular form. If this is granted, then this form actually behaves in a completely predictable way, following the normal pattern of /w/ nasalization.

Now that all of the reduplicated forms relevant to /w/ nasalization in Southern Paiute are accounted for in the present analysis, we can compare this analysis to the one offered by McCarthy and Prince (1995:349-351). The modular and derivational analysis developed here is superior to the Optimality Theory analysis presented by McCarthy and Prince based on empirical coverage, the phonetic vs. phonological sources of [w], and derived environment effects.

The metric of empirical coverage clearly favors the present analysis over the one offered by McCarthy and Prince since they do not discuss the inserted [w]s other than stating that they believe these segments to be a "phonetic matter" (McCarthy and Prince 1995:350, fn. 79). While the present analysis basically agrees that the inserted [w]s are a late phonological process or even a purely phonetic mater, the issue here is that within a modular model of phonology the distinction between phonological and phonetic matters is relatively clear but in a nonmodular parallel model of grammar as espoused by Optimality Theory the distinction between phonetic and phonological matters is not clear at all. Given the grammatical assumptions in McCarthy and Prince (1995), the proposed surface constraint *VwV will treat all intervocalic [w]s as violations, regardless of their source. This issue must be addressed before an equivalent amount of empirical coverage can be credited to both analyses. The exceptional forms must also be provided an explanation and this task also appears to be a difficult one since Optimality Theory (Prince and Smolensky 1993) does not contain a method of marking exceptional forms (Halle 1998).

The second issue of distinguishing between underlying /w/ and inserted [w] also favors the derivational analysis because this distinction is opaque. The basic assumption of a derivational model of phonology is that there is an ordering of processes. Given this fact, ordering the insertion of [w] after the /w/ nasalization process is claimed to be a completely natural way of explaining why inserted [w]s do not undergo the /w/ nasalization process. Optimality Theory will has difficulty in accounting for opacity effects and would require some approach to opacity such as sympathy theory (McCarthy 2000) to account for Southern Paiute. Explanations that result from the simple ordering of processes present strong arguments in favor of modular and/or derivational models of grammar. Southern Paiute /w/ nasalization is a case of this.

The final argument against the McCarthy and Prince (1995) analysis of Southern Paiute is the Derived Environment Condition that is crucial in characterizing the behavior of /w/ nasalization. It is very clear that Sapir (1930) identified this process only with morphologically complex forms but McCarthy and Prince do not address this fact at all. Nor do they provide any evidence to support their interpretation of the facts. The claim that the underapplication of /w/ nasalization in reduplicated forms results from a highly ranked base reduplicant faithfulness constraint denies that there is any connection between the behavior of reduplicated forms and the behavior of morphologically complex forms. There is no prediction to be made from one case to the other in the correspondence model analysis of Southern Paiute. In contrast, by placing a Derived Environment Condition on the application of /w/ nasalization, the derivational analysis proposed here immediately predicts the underapplication of the reduplicated forms. As seen in the Chumash /l/ deletion example, a Derived Environment Condition predicts that the process in question should underapply in reduplicated constructions just as long as there is no prespecified phonological material associated with the reduplicated loop. Southern Paiute further confirms this fact. Based on the predictions that can be made from the utilization of a Derived Environment Condition the derivational analysis is superior to the Optimality Theory based analysis.

To conclude this section, the interaction of reduplication and /w/ nasalization in Southern Paiute has been investigated. The general pattern of the distribution of [w] and [ŋʷ] derived from /w/ can be accounted for by placing a Derived Environment Condition on the

/w/ nasalization process and by proposing a separate process that inserts [w] to break up hiatus of /uV/ in the postcyclic block of rules. Contrary to the claims made by McCarthy and Prince (1995), there is no need for any sort of correspondence or Identity Constraint (Wilbur 1973) to account for the data in Southern Paiute. In comparing the McCarthy and Prince (1995) analysis and the one developed here, we can conclude that Southern Paiute presents another case that favors a modular and derivational analysis utilizing the representations proposed for reduplication in this section.

2.3   The role of the derivation

Section 2.2 has dealt with cases of over- and underapplication of phonological rules in reduplicative forms. All of these cases of reduplication and rule interaction crucially have a rule applying before the linearization process occurs. The result from this ordering are cases of opacity where it appears a rule has applied or not applied for no apparent reason. In contrast to this, there are cases of interaction between phonological rules and reduplication where a given rule only applies when the environment for the rule is surface true. This situation is referred to as *normal application* and it occurs when a rule applies after linearization has occurred. Since linearization has caused the repetition of parts of a looped phonological structure, there is no identity relation between the repeated regions. Consequently, since there is no identity relation between regions of repeated segments, rules that apply to these phonological representations can cause the "base" and "reduplicant" to become different.

An excellent example of normal application of phonological rules comes from Korean. The relevant facts are that Korean has postcyclic rules of cluster simplification, nasal assimilation, palatalization, and tensification. The application of these rules after linearization has occurred leads to a substantial divergence between the two copies of the stem. Consider the example in (42) from Martin (1992:100).

(42) a. moks-moks-i [moŋmokʃ'i] 'in portions, in shares'

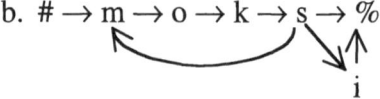

b. # → m → o → k → s → %

i

c. # → m → o → k → s → m → o → k → s → i → %

d.
	moksmoksi
syllabification	(mok)s(mok)(si)
tensification	(mok)s(mok)(s'i)
cluster simplification	(mok)(mok)(s'i)
nasal assimilation	(moŋ)(mok)(s'i)
palatalization	(moŋ)(mok)(ʃ'i)
etc.	[moŋmokʃ'i]

(42a) presents two representations, one indicating the reduplication of the stem, *moks-moks-i*, and one presenting the phonetic form of this compound. The disparity between these two representations shows that reduplication in this form is not readily apparent. (42b) shows the representation that is built by the morphology. (42c) shows the representation that is produced from linearizing (42b) and (42d) shows the rules that apply to the postlinearization representation.

For the Korean example in (42), linearization occurs exactly at the juncture between the cyclic and postcyclic blocks of rules. Mester (1988) argues that this is *the* fixed ordering of linearization presented by universal grammar. The fixed ordering of cyclic rules > linearization > postcyclic rules creates the simple typology of rule reduplication interaction presented in (43).

(43)

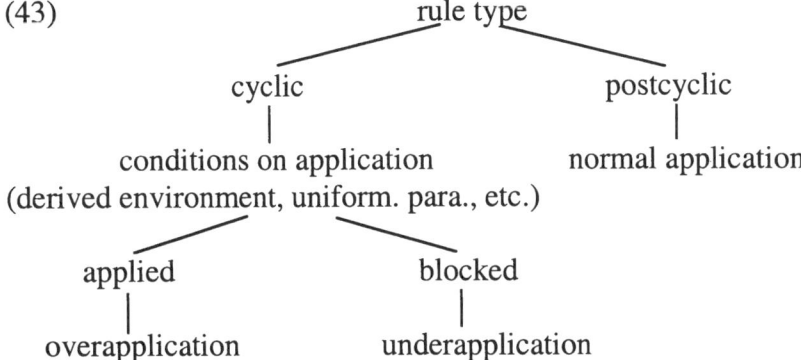

rule type

cyclic

postcyclic

conditions on application
(derived environment, uniform. para., etc.)

normal application

applied

blocked

overapplication

underapplication

This simple typology reflects the claims that Mester makes that only certain rules behave exceptionally in reduplicated structures. Mester (1988:248) states that,

> "...Tier Conflation linearizes the structure. This makes a clear prediction for rules which follow [linearization], in particular for all post[cyclic] rules: They should never have overapplication or underapplication effects; rather, they should always apply in the normal way wherever their linear context is met, and reduplicated forms should not be special in any way, as far as post[cyclic] rules are concerned".

The typology in (43) is referred to as "simple" because the claims made by this model are not always surface true. Depending on what conditions are placed on the application of a cyclic rule different opacities will obscure this typology. All conditions on a rule's application will cause the alternation between the appearances of normal application and either overapplication or underapplication depending on whether the multiple environments that a segment appears in are identical along a given dimension or not. If the multiple environments are the same for a crucial condition on a rule then the surface result will be normal application regardless of rule type. It is only when the multiple environments of a prelinearization reduplicated form are different that overapplication and underapplication effects will be observed.

The Uniformity Parameter causes the appearance of an alternation between normal application and opaque application. If the Uniformity Parameter is set to *off*, surface forms will alternate between normal application and overapplication. The Malay case in section 2.2.1 shows this alternation with the data discussed giving examples of the overapplication and forms that do not trigger the nasalization rule at all (e.g. *buku* 'book', *buku-buku* 'books') providing the cases of normal application. The Akan example from the same section indicates that the surface data will show alternations between normal application and underapplication if the Uniformity Parameter is set to *on*. If the source of exceptional behavior is the Uniformity Parameter we expect the opacity that results to be directly related to the structural description of the process in question.

Exceptional behavior caused by the Derived Environment Condition will create opacities based on the morphological structures of words. The examples analyzed in this chapter from Chaha, Chumash, and Southern Paiute provide examples of the patterns of opacity that result from the Derived Environment Condition. The Derived Environment Condition shows normal application in morphologically complex forms and opacity in morphologically simplex forms. Note that this pattern is complicated by whether a reduplicated structure contains segmental material or not. If there is some prespecified segmental material associated with the reduplicative loop then the reduplicated form will act as a morphologically complex form. If there is no segmental material added by the reduplicative morpheme then the resulting reduplicated form will act as if it were morphologically simplex. The Chaha example shows that the pattern of surface opacity is flipped when the Derived Environment Condition requires application only in nonderived environments. This indicates that the predictions about whether a reduplicated structure counts as a derived or nonderived environment based on segmental material contained in the reduplicative morpheme are true.

The simple typology in (43) can be further obscured by the possibility of multiple applications of the linearization process. Examples of the overapplication and underapplication of late applying (postlexical in Kiparsky's terms) rules in Kiparsky (1986) receive a natural explanation if there is the late addition of reduplicative morphology which would trigger another application of linearization after a word has already been linearized. The idea of multiple linearization coincides with theoretical arguments made by Uriagereka (1999) and empirical data presented by Lidz (1999). A brief summary of the relevant points of Uriagereka (1999) is that an entire phrase marker is not necessarily linearized as a single piece or at a single point of a derivation. A derivation will cause smaller parts of a phrase structure to be spelled-out and passed onto the phonological component at different points in the derivation. The relevance of multiple spell-out is clear when the phenomenon of echo reduplication in Kannada (Emeneau 1938, Lidz 1999) is considered. The importance of the data presented by Lidz is that an entire phrasal category is being reduplicated. Consider (44) and note that echo reduplication in Kannada overwrites a prespecified syllable *gii-* on the first syllable of what is reduplicated.

(44) a. nannu   baa*gil-annu*   *much-id-e*   **giigilannu muchide**
         I-NOM   door-ACC   close-PST-1S   **RED**
         anta   heeLa-beeDa
         that   say-PROH
         'Don't say that I closed the door or did related activities.'

    b. pustav-annu   mee*jin-a meele*   **giijina meele**   nooD-id-e
        book-ACC   table-gen on   **RED**   see-PST-1S
        'I saw the book on the table and in related places.'

Italics in (44) indicates what the base is for reduplication and boldface indicates what the reduplicant is. Notice that both reduplicated regions begin with the prespecified *gii-* morpheme. In (44a) an entire verb phrase is being reduplicated and (44b) shows a prepositional phrase being reduplicated. Additionally, smaller units (single morphemes, groups of morphemes, etc.) can be reduplicated by echo reduplication in Kannada (Lidz 1999).

The existence of data that shows a single type of reduplication affecting different sizes of syntactic structures provides strong evidence that the overall structure of a derivation allows for multiple applications of linearization which can obscure the claims made by the typology in (43). This indicates that to fully comprehend how reduplication interacts with the phonology, especially the surface apparent results of this interaction, the complete derivation of morpho-syntactic features to phonetic form must be understood. This is well beyond the present state of linguistic theory but the model of reduplication presented in this chapter provides a clear guide to how future research on reduplication can contribute to this goal.

2.4   Summary

This chapter has argued for the explicit representation of precedence in phonological representations. This proposal allows subtly more complex phonological structures to be built by the morphological component than have previously been considered. The small amount of additional complexity includes the possibility that a single segment can immediately precede or follow more than one other segment. Just this situation obtains in forms that show reduplication according to the claim that reduplication is the result of a loop in a phonological representation. Whenever there is a loop in a phonological representation, the beginning and end of the loop will have segments that occur in multiple environments. Segments appearing in multiple environments allow a new and deeper understanding of the interaction between phonological rules and reduplication.

Prior to this work, the view that reduplication can cause exceptional behavior of phonological rules has been an accepted assumption in generative phonology since Wilbur (1973) first identified overapplication and underapplication effects. McCarthy and Prince (1995) diverge from this position by claiming that the terminology of overapplication and underapplication is a relic of previous rule based systems. Instead, McCarthy and Prince (1993b) account for the interaction between phonological processes and reduplication by introducing the concept of correspondence. One of the crucial aspects of correspondence theory (McCarthy and Prince 1995) is that there are multiple different correspondences between the input and output, the base and the reduplicant, the input and the reduplicant, etc. This allows the behavior of reduplicated forms to be accounted for by a cophonology that is encoded by base/reduplicant correspondence. This set of constraints that only affects the relationship between the base and the reduplicant can be ranked differently with respect to fixed markedness constraints (Prince and Smolensky 1993) than other correspondence constraints (input/output, output/output, etc.). It is the discrepancy between the ranking of base/reduplicant correspondence constraints and input/output correspondence constraints that drives the success of Optimality Theory in accounting for reduplication. This approach is equivalent to stipulating a special reduplication specific cophonology though and this point calls into question whether any real advance in the understanding of reduplication has been provided by Optimality Theory.

The view of the interaction between reduplication and phonological processes presented in this chapter is inherently different from both Wilbur's and McCarthy and Prince's. Simply stated, there is no special status given to reduplication in the phonological component. Cases that McCarthy and Prince (1995) present as evidence against derivational models of reduplication have been insightfully accounted for given the derivational approach presented here. Throughout all of these analyses there is never any implementation or adoption of a reduplication specific mechanism to explain the application (or non-application) of a given process. The analyses explain the interaction between reduplication and a phonological rule by using established principles of generative phonology. The only novel claim that is required is the addition of a Uniformity Parameter on rules that indicates a rule's sensitivity to multiple environments. This parameter is crucial in the accounts of Malay and Akan presented here. We must note that this parameter exists on all phonological rules and therefore it is not a reduplication specific mechanism. An analysis of infixation in chapter 3 will make this point clear. It is just a fluke of the representations of reduplication that makes this parameter appear to be reduplication specific.

The claim that reduplication does not act exceptionally in the phonological component is an argument in favor of this approach over all previous models of reduplication. By eliminating the special status of reduplication in phonology, we reach a deeper understanding of not only reduplication but also of phonology in general. This point segues into the next argument in favor of the approach to reduplication presented here.

This argument is based on Prosodic Morphology (McCarthy and Prince 1986, 1993b). The main goal of Prosodic Morphology (McCarthy and Prince 1986) is, "[t]o explain properties of morphology/phonology dependency in terms of *independent, general* properties" (McCarthy and Prince 1994b:B1). Additionally, McCarthy and Prince state, "Our goal, which is the same as the goal of all linguistic theory, is to achieve greater empirical coverage with fewer resources–maybe with no resources at all that are specific to the domain under investigation" (McCarthy and Prince 1994b:B13). The main connection between these goals and correspondence theory is that McCarthy and Prince (1995) claim that correspondence is the basic phonological resource. Consequently, if all of phonology can then be accounted for in terms of correspondence effects, the goal of Prosodic Morphology is met since there are no process specific mechanisms present in the phonology.

At one level, correspondence theory achieves the above goals. The issue of how different correspondence relationships affect this goal needs to be addressed though. McCarthy and Prince (1995: 264) allow, "separate (and therefore separately rankable) constraints for each correspondence relation (input/output, base/reduplicant, etc)". Furthermore, "...each reduplicative affix has its own correspondence relation, so that in a language with several reduplicative affixes there can be several distinct, separately rankable constraints of the MAX_{BR} type, etc." (McCarthy and Prince 1995:265). This situation indicates that correspondence is the general mechanism that is the foundation of phonology but that correspondence is manipulable on a morpheme by morpheme basis. As mentioned earlier, the ability to rank different correspondence relations in different manners is equivalent to building cophonologies into a grammar. This approach makes the inherent claim that reduplication is so special that it requires its own sub-grammar and ranking of constraints in order to be accounted for. So while McCarthy and Prince (1995) is successful in deriving reduplication effects from the general idea of correspondence, there is still a large element of process specific mechanism built into their analysis of reduplication.

In contrast, the proposals here do not add any new reduplication specific mechanisms to generative phonology. These proposals only clarify how precedence is represented in phonology and how this representation changes via a linearization process. All of reduplication can now be accounted for solely by serial process ordering. Cases where there appears to be anomalous application of phonological processes are dealt with within the phonology as normal rule application (or non-application as case may be). Overapplication and underapplication effects are explained as cases of opacity where a phonological environment has either been created or destroyed after a process has had the opportunity to apply. This view places reduplication firmly within the umbra of explanation provided by classical generative phonology.

By providing analyses that are equivalent or superior in explanation of the data presented by McCarthy and Prince (1995) to argue against serial models of phonology, the model of reduplication developed in this chapter allows an argument based on opacity to be presented against Optimality Theory. Put simply, opacity effects cause serious empirical and conceptual problems for Optimality Theory. McCarthy (2000) outlines the empirical problems that standard Optimality Theory has in accounting for opacity effects and to remedy this situation, McCarthy proposes the idea of *sympathy*. Sympathy provides a solution to some opacity effects but Ito and Mester (1999) and Odden (2000) argue that sympathy is incapable of conceptually accounting for all cases of opacity. Furthermore, Kaisse (2000) and Idsardi and Kim (to appear) both show that sympathy theory makes wrong predications about cases of multiple opacity. Consequently, these examples highlight empirical problems for sympathy theory and Optimality Theory. An approach to phonology that can adequately account for both opacity effects and reduplication is to be preferred over theories that can only account for one of these phenomena.

The reduction of overapplication and underapplication effects to cases of opacity is one of the strongest points in favor of the proposals in this chapter. The full integration of the model of reduplication into a modular approach to morphology and phonology results in an overall system that has no reduplication specific mechanisms which is another strong argument in favor of this approach. The final attribute of the model of reduplication developed here that presents a strong reason for its adoption is the explanation of identity effects that is provided. The two repeated regions of phonological material that are present in reduplicated structures are similar because they are a single entity for a part of the derivation. At a point in the derivation, this identity is severed due to the linearization process and this allows phonological processes to apply and alter the now separate phonological regions. When placed within a derivational model of phonology, this type of interaction between phonological processes is the normal case and is to be expected. We can thus conclude that the model of reduplication presented in this chapter is the first one to provide an adequate phonological explanation for the interaction of phonological rules and reduplication including cases of backcopying. The model presented here is adequate because it derives the behavior of reduplication from general principles of generative phonology.

Chapter 3
Precedence in morphology

This chapter discusses some of the more important morphological issues that are relevant to the construction of the phonological representations that were assumed in chapter 2. To begin, a brief summary of Distributed Morphology is presented to highlight the differences between the morphological assumptions present in the model of reduplication developed here and the assumptions made by other models of reduplication. Following this, the implications for the phonological representations of affixes of the proposals in chapter 2 are outlined. This leads to an analysis of reduplicative affixes that claims that they are equivalent to other affixes in phonological material but differ from simple affixation in a fundamental way. The changes to a phonological structure caused by a reduplicative affix are accomplished via a readjustment rule instead of the spell-out of the phonological material of a specific morpheme. The fact that reduplication is not the primary exponent of a morpho-syntactic feature supports the readjustment rule approach to reduplication. To support the claim about the similarity between the phonological resources used by affixation and reduplication, analyses of infixation and melodic overwriting effects in reduplication are presented. An explanation for the surface appearance of reduplicative templates also results from the precedence information that is contained in a reduplicative affix as analyses of different templates shows.

3.1   A modular grammar

Prior to Wilbur (1973) it was assumed that there was a strong division between the morphology and phonology. The evidence adduced by Wilbur has been a strong motivation to weaken (or even eliminate) the modularity between morphology and phonology. The culmination of this trend is in Optimality Theory where there is no division between the morphology and phonology. A non-modular approach to morphology and phonology is explicitly advocated in Optimality Theory due to the consistency of exponence (McCarthy and Prince 1993b:20-21) and the use of generalized alignment constraints (McCarthy and Prince 1993a). Consistency of exponence states that the GEN function in Optimality Theory is incapable of altering the morphological affiliation of phonological material. Since GEN is unable to alter the morphological affiliation of phonological material, whatever morphological information is present in the input will be present in the phonological output contrary to modularity. The use of generalized alignment constraints also requires morphological information to be contained in the output representations that are evaluated in tableau since this type of constraint can require a morphological and phonological category to coincide. If morphological information were not present in the output there would be no way to evaluate or possibly satisfy this kind of generalized alignment constraint. It is thus clear that Optimality Theory employs a non-modular morphology and phonology.[1]

Given the modifications to the representation of precedence in chapter 2, the interaction between reduplication and phonological rules no longer requires a non-modular approach. A modular approach to reduplication is attractive not only because it would operate within a more constrained model of grammar that limits the interaction of morphology and phonology but also because it satisfies the principle of full interpretation (Chomsky 1995). The principle of full interpretation with respect to phonology limits phonological representations to only contain representations that reflect sensorimotor information (Chomsky 1995:27). Therefore, spell-out is a trading relation, sounds for morphemes.

The consideration of modularity and full interpretation leads to the desire to situate the present model of reduplication within a model of morphology that satisfies these ideals. Distributed Morphology (Halle and Marantz 1993, 1994, Noyer 1997, among others) provides a theory of morphology where these goals are achievable. The main attractive feature of Distributed Morphology is that it is modular theory of grammar where a separate morphology module precedes a separate phonology module. This position returns to a strong view of the separation between morphology and phonology that has been abandoned in Optimality Theory. This approach allows the separate morphological and phonological aspects of reduplication to be relegated to corresponding separate modules where module specific principles can be used to explain reduplication.

A second aspect of Distributed Morphology that provides a crucial insight into the understanding of reduplication is the idea of readjustment rules. Readjustment rules are rules that can modify the phonological or morpho-syntactic features of a given morpheme. These rules reside in the morphology module and a crucial aspect to them is that they never provide the primary exponence of a particular morpheme (Noyer 1997). Distributed Morphology takes the position that any secondary exponence of a particular morpheme is accomplished via readjustment rules. The issue of secondary exponence is important to the understanding of the morphological aspects of reduplication because reduplication in itself is the secondary exponence of a given morpho-syntactic feature in many cases. The data in (45) presents cases where an affix is accompanied by reduplication in the stem that the affix attaches to.

(45) a. Bella Coola Diminutives
(Nater 1984, Bagemihl 1989)

qayt	'hat'	qa-qayt-i	'toadstool' (Diminutive)
silin	'kidney'	sil-slin-i	Diminutive
t'ixɬala	'robin'	ʔi-t'ixɬala-y	Diminutive
qax	'rabit'	qaax-qx-i	Diminutive
sum	'trousers'	su-sum-ii	Diminutive
stn	'tree'	s-tn-tn-ii	Diminutive

b. Tagalog Occupational Noun Prefix /maŋ/
(Carrier 1979:66)

mam-ba-bayan	'citizen'
man-la-laroʔ	'player'
maŋ-gu-gupit	'barber'
maŋ-ha-halal	'voter'

    c. Ilokano Progressive Reduplication
    (Hayes and Abad 1989)

?ag-bas-basa	'be reading'
?ag-da-dait	'be sewing'
?ag-ad-adal	'be studying'
?ag-tak-takder	'be standing'

The data in (45) show cases where reduplicative patterns have additional morphology that can not be semantically separated. Bella Coola, (45a), has forms that have a diminutive suffix, *-i*, in addition to reduplication. Tagalog, (45b), has reduplication patterns that only occur in the presence of the Occupational Noun prefix /maŋ/. A similar pattern obtains in Ilokano, (45c), where the progressive is formed by adding a prefix /?ag/ in conjunction with reduplication of the first syllable.

    Another aspect of reduplication that is crucial to understanding it is the fact that many reduplication patterns are polysemous in a given language. The important idea here is that if an overt change to a form appears in different forms with different meanings, then it is not the process in question that is causing the change in meaning, something else is.[2] This is similar to Leiber's idea that morpholexical rule relations cannot alter the features of a stem. Lieber (1980:42) states, "...unlike other rules of word formation, they [morpholexical rules] do not change category, alter subcategorization, or add to, change or subtract from semantic content, however that is characterized". This characteristic of reduplication can be seen in the examples in (46).

(46) a. Bella Coola CVC reduplications
      (Nater 1984, Bagemihl 1989)

yałk	'do too much'	yał-yałk	Continuative
milix^w	'bear berry'	mil-milix^w	'plant of the bear berry'
ck^w-ał	'heavy feet'	c-k^{w}ał-k^{w}ał	'to walk heavily'
x^{w}alc	'to melt'	x^{w}al-x^{w}alc	'solder'
suca	'hand'	suc-suca	'both hands'
stan	'mother'	s-tan-tan-mts	'all female ancestors...'
culta	'fire drill'	cul-culm	'to start a fire with...'

b. Chumash (C)CVC- reduplications
(Wash 1995)

wot?	'chief'	wot?wot?	Plural
q?o?y	'olivella'	q?oyq?o?y	'(quant. of) olivella'
nuk?a	'where; when'	nuknuk?a?	'places'
pak?a	'one'	pakpak?a	'one by one'

c. Nakanai CVCV reduplications
(Spaelti 1997:76)

raga-raga	'jumping'/Cont. Habituative Verbs
muluga-luga	'to be first...'/Concrete Nouns
bolo-bolo	'many pigs'/Collective Plural Nouns
ilima-lima	'five'/Distributive Numerals

The data from Nakanai in (46c) are particularly clear support for the view that reduplication patterns can be polysemous. Spaelti (1997) explicates the distribution between the meaning and pattern in Nakanai.

"Reduplication in Nakanai does have a large number of different uses: marking of non-singular agreement, continuative habituative mood, derivation of intransitive verbs from transitives, formation of collective plural nouns, concrete nouns, and distributive numerals. However, the shape of the reduplicated form is independent of the usage. All usages occur with any of the patterns." (Spaelti 1997:75)

This situation is the best possible evidence that reduplication is not necessarily the primary exponence of a particular morpheme.

The fact that reduplication acts as a secondary exponence of some morphemes does not require that all reduplication patterns have additional overt morphology. Morpho-syntactic features that do not have any phonological material associated with them that trigger a readjustment rule will account for cases when a given reduplication pattern is polysemous. This approach posits a zero morph that will trigger the appropriate readjustment rule. The analysis of strong verb formation in English argued for by Halle and Marantz (1994:124-138) presents a case where a zero morph triggers the application of a readjustment rule. Consider the exam-

ples of the past tense forms of some strong verbs in English presented in (47).

(47)   *present*   *past*
    a. steal   stole + Ø
       sing   sang + Ø
       fall   fell + Ø
       bind   bound + Ø

    b. leave   lef + t
       buy   bough + t
       tell   tol + d
       do   di + d

The verbs in (47) primarily differ in whether the past tense morpheme is realized with phonological material or not. The forms in
(47a) are strong verbs in English and thus have the phonologically
null realization of the past tense morpheme. In addition to this zero
morph a readjustment rule affects the vowel in the morpheme
changing its quality. The forms in (47b) also under go readjustment
rules that affect the vowels present in the morphemes (and changes
/v/ to /f/ in *leave~left*) but they have either /d/ or /t/ as the
phonological spell-out of the past tense morpheme. Because the
spell-out of the past tense morpheme is variable between (47a) and
(47b) we can conclude that it is the morpho-syntactic features of the
past tense morpheme and not the phonological content that is triggering the readjustment rule.

    Since readjustment rules are triggered by the morpho-syntactic
features of a morpheme, the phonological material associated with a
morpheme that triggers a readjustment rule should be excluded
from the range of the readjustment. This is supported by the behavior of readjustment rules that create reduplicated forms. Consider the example of light syllable (CV) reduplication from Ilokano
(Hayes and Abad 1989:357) in (48).

(48) dáʔit   'to sew'   ʔagin-da-dáʔit 'pretend to sew'
      sáŋit   'to cry'   ʔagin-sa-sáŋit 'pretend to cry'

| tugáw | 'to sit' | ʔag-tu-tugáw | 'sits restfully' |
| sála | 'to dance' | ʔag-sa-sála | 'characteristically dances' |

Light syllable reduplication in Ilokano co-occurs with a prefix in the examples in (48). Importantly these prefixes are not reduplicated so given the approximate morphological structure in (49) and cyclic spell-out of morphemes, a derivation of the form in (50) results. The [+RR] feature in (49) below *ʔagin* indicates that this affix triggers a readjustment rule.

(49)

```
              /\
             /  \
        ʔagin    root
        [+RR]     |
               dáʔit
```

(50) a. # → d → á → ʔ → i → t → %

b. # → d → á → ʔ → i → t → %

c.

→ d → á → ʔ → i → t → %

ʔ → a → g → i → n

The derivation in (50) indicates that the root is spelled-out first. When it comes time to spell-out the affix, the readjustment rule triggered by the affix applies to the root first as shown in (50b). After the readjustment rule has applied, the affix is then spelled out as in (50c) and this ordering correctly predicts that reduplication triggered by an affix, whether this affix is phonologically null or not, should only affect previously spelled-out phonological material.

All of the polysemous reduplication patterns presented in (46) are examples of reduplication triggered by zero morphs. Presumably in these patterns, each separate semantic distinction is associated with a particular morpho-syntactic feature and the polysemy arises from the fact that these different morphemes trigger the same readjustment rule that causes reduplication. It is very difficult to find an exact one-to-one correspondence between a semantic distinction and a single reduplication pattern without additional morphology in any language. This situation indicates that it is likely that all reduplication patterns result from a readjustment rule and that reduplication is never a morpheme in and of itself. In other words, where a reduplication pattern is not accompanied by additional phonological changes the primary exponence of the morphosyntactic or semantic features is a zero morph which causes reduplication as a readjustment.

3.2   The concatenation of morphemes

The new representations proposed for the phonological module in chapter 2 have major implications for the understanding of what the phonological aspects of morphemes are and how morphemes are concatenated. The notions of root, prefix, suffix, infix, etc. can be directly encoded in the phonological material that is associated with a morpho-syntactic feature.

We will pursue a model of morpheme concatenation that shares ideas with the containment model proposed by Prince and Smolensky (1993) and proposals made in Noyer (1997b). Some of these traits have already been seen in the phonological structures utilized in chapter 2. The main aspect of the model of morpheme concatenation being developed is that morphology will be primarily structure building. This view exploits the ability to build complex phonological representations that only increase in complexity and phonological material when morphemes are added. The characteristic that information is not destroyed by the addition of morphemes is what makes this model similar to the containment model of Prince and Smolensky. The characteristic that morphemes can only add phonological material[3] is shared with Noyer (1997b).

Let us consider some examples of prefixation and suffixation. We see that the word *unlock* consists of a free root *lock* and a bound prefix *un-*. All of the aspects of prefix, free and bound can be directly encoded by what information is contained in the precedence relations in the phonological representations, as seen in (51).

(51) a. lock   /lak/   *free root*

$$\# \rightarrow l \rightarrow a \rightarrow k \rightarrow \%$$

b. un   /ʌn/   *bound prefix*

$$\# \rightarrow ʌ \rightarrow n \rightarrow \{X\}$$

When we recall the representations presented throughout chapter 2, we immediately see a difference in the representations for *lock* in (51a) and *un-* in (51b). Specifically, (51a) is a well-formed phonological representation that has a complete transitive precedence ordering from # to %. (51b) is not well formed in this respect because there is no end point for this phonological representation (it lacks a %). This difference of well-formedness between (51a) and (51b) shows the difference between a phonologically free and bound item. Affixes are phonologically bound and will have variables that specify how they are concatenated with other morphemes. The presence of a variable that defines a precedence relation is indicated in (51b) by the bracketed material.

Precedence variables that are part of the phonological representation of affixes define a particular segment that will satisfy a specified precedence relationship. The precedence relationship that ends the prefix in (51b) is not specific enough to actually concatenate it with the root in (51a) because not enough precedence information has been given. (52) presents a typology of morphemes based on what phonological information is present.

(52) *type*	*beginning*	*end*
free	$\# \rightarrow$	$\rightarrow \%$
prefix	$\# \rightarrow$	$\{\# \rightarrow \_\_\}$
suffix	$\{\_\_ \rightarrow \%\}$	$\rightarrow \%$
other	$\{X\}$	$\{Y\}$

A morpheme that is phonologically free will have a precedence structure that has both a beginning and an end which will allow it to be linearized. A prefix is a morpheme that has a specified beginning but has a variable that specifies that it precedes the beginning of some other phonological material. A suffix is the opposite case where a variable specifies that it follows some other phonological material but the suffix will end a precedence graph. Any morpheme that contains a variable that does not concatenate with some other phonological material to discharge the variable will crash during the linearization process and this explains their boundedness. It should be noted that morphemes can be bound for other reasons than just phonological ones through restrictions on morpho-syntactic features.

There is one type of morpheme left in (52) under the name "other" that has variables that specify both the beginning and end of it. This type of morpheme covers infixes and reduplication with the difference among them being what the relationship between the two variables is. In general, infixes will have a beginning precedence variable that precedes the ending precedence variable when the infix is concatenated with a stem. Reduplication has the opposite relationship between its precedence variables with the beginning variable specifying a point that temporally follows the point described by the ending variable. Presence or lack of segmental material does not distinguish between infixes and reduplicative affixes and this will be discussed in section 3.3.

Due to the possible complexity added to the phonological representation of a morpheme, we will standardize the presentation of the precedence information in a morpheme. If a precedence relationship is distinct and non-variable, then the now familiar arrow that indicates the relationship of *precedes* will be used. If a precedence relationship is variable in that it describes some position of a precedence structure then either *begin* or *end* will be used in the representation of the morpheme. The description of this precedence variable will then be presented in two formats. The first format will utilize *begin* and *end* in the representation of the affix with structural descriptions for *begin* and *end* variables presented below the affix when necessary. The second format will present the morpheme concatenation as a precedence graph with dotted arrows to indicate what precedence variables have been discharged. These two formats are notational variants that allow different aspects of the concatenation process to be highlighted. Consider the examples of this layout with the English prefix *un-* presented in (53a,b) and suffix *-ish* in (53c,d).

(53) a. $\# \to \Lambda \to n \to end$ b. $\# \to X$
        $end:$ $\# \to \_\_$ $\uparrow$
                                  $\# \to \Lambda \to n$

    c. $begin \to \iota \to \int \to \%$ c. $X \to \%$
       $begin:$ $\_\_ \to \%$ $\uparrow$
                                   $\iota \to \int \to \%$

Returning to the example of prefixation presented by *unlock*, (54) shows the phonological structure that results from concatenating *un-* and *lock* given the representation for *un-* given in (53a).

(54) $\# \to l \to a \to k \to \%$
     $\downarrow$ $\uparrow$
     $\Lambda \to n$

Two things should be noted of the concatenation process. The first is that there is only a single beginning and end present in any precedence structure. Thus, multiple instances of either # or % will collapse into a single entity that combines the precedence information from them. This seen in (54) where both /l/ and /ʌ/ follow #. The other notable process is the substitution of the precedence variable in the affix with the segment that satisfies this variable. This is also seen in (54) where /n/ precedes /l/ since /l/ satisfies the environment of the variable. A precedence variable of a morpheme can not be satisfied by any segment that is part of the morpheme. This prevents /ʌ/ from satisfying the precedence variable which would result in /n/ preceding /ʌ/.

The concatenation of morphemes respects the derivational history of a formative because of the principle that gives more importance to recently added material. The addition of multiple prefixes or suffixes has the effect of placing additional affixes to the outside of previously added ones because of this principle. Consider (55) which shows the step by step concatenation of *boyishness*.

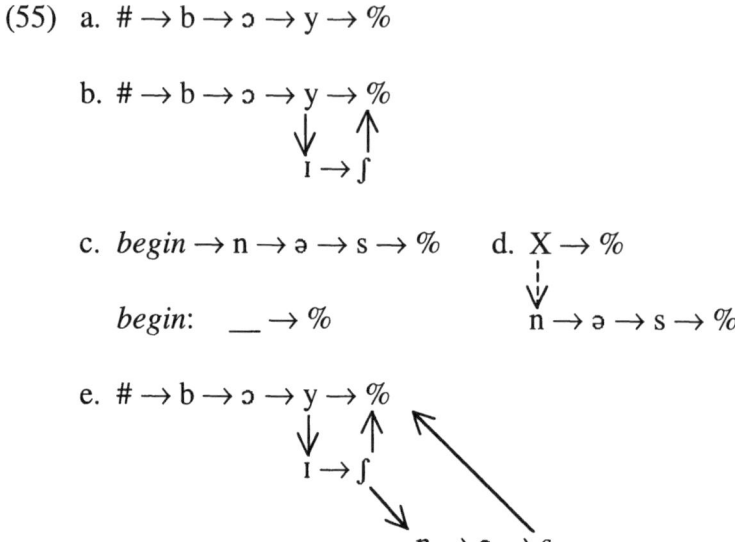

(55) a. # → b → ɔ → y → %

   b. # → b → ɔ → y → %

   c. *begin* → n → ə → s → %   d. X → %

      begin: __ → %   n → ə → s → %

   e. # → b → ɔ → y → %

      n → ə → s

(55a) shows the root and (55b) shows the concatenation of *-ish* to this root given the representation of *-ish* in (53b). Concatenation here is the same as the example in (54) except a suffix has been added instead of a prefix. (55c,d) presents the phonological representation for *-ness* and (55e) shows the precedence structure that results from the additional concatenation of *-ness* to (55b). The only issue here is to make sure that the precedence variable for *-ness* is satisfied by the end of *-ish* and not the root. If the precedence variable of *-ness* was discharged by the root, a decision would have to be made by the linearization process to only linearize one of the two suffixes. This problem is remedied by the principle that makes sure that the identifiable end or beginning of a formative reflects the most recently added phonological material.[4]

3.3   Infixes and reduplication

The discussion of prefixes and suffixes in section 2 of this chapter only illuminates the rudimentary aspects of the precedence variables that are used in the phonological representations of morphemes. Infixes and reduplication show the full possibilities of precedence variables not only because of the presence of two variables in these kinds of morphemes but also due to the types of precedence variables instantiated. Prefixes and suffixes only make reference to the first and last segment of a formative in their precedence variables but more exotic variables are utilized in natural languages.

To begin the investigation of the range of possible precedence variables, we will examine infixation in Sundanese. This pattern of infixation provides evidence for a very common type of infixation and for the complex precedence structures built by the morphology.

Sundanese (Robins 1957, Anderson 1980) has an infix, *-ar-/-al-*, that is placed into the root directly after a word initial consonant. Data supporting the infixing behavior of this affix is presented in (56). Note that the /r/ of the affix dissimilates to /l/ if there is an /r/ that follows in the root.

(56)   moekən   'to dry'   m-ar-oekən   Plural
       ɲaur   'to say'   ɲ-al-aur   Plural
       niis   'to cool oneself'   n-ar-iis   Plural
       ɲaho   'to know'   ɲ-ar-aho   Plural

The phonological representation of the affix /ar/ with the appropriate precedence variables is presented in (57a,b).

(57)   a. *begin* → a → r → *end*   b.   a → r
                                                      ⋀   ⋁
           begin: # → __   # → X ... X
           end: __ |
                         | # *   line 0
                        # *   line 0

c. $\# \rightarrow n \rightarrow i \rightarrow i \rightarrow s \rightarrow \%$
$$a \rightarrow r$$

Since /ar/ is an infix we find both *begin* and *end* precedence variables in (57a,b). (57c) shows the precedence structure that results from concatenating /ar/ with a root. The structure that is built by the morphology in (57c) indicates that there is a detour from the /n/ into the infix /ar/ and then back to /i/ in the root. This detour is accomplished by the variables that specify the behavior of the infix. The *begin* precedence variable in (57a) states that /ar/ follows whatever segment begins the root. The *end* precedence variable in (57a) requires more access to the phonology of the form in that it specifies that the affix precedes the first vowel of the formative. The "first vowel" can be determined by examining the metrical grid (Idsardi 1992) for the formative, locating the first line 0 mark and then identifying which segment this grid mark is associated to. The morphology module must have access to the metrical module in order to account for allomorphy conditioned by stress as in the English suffix -*al* that creates deverbal nominals. This suffix only attaches to stress final stems (i.e. *remóv-al*, *betráy-al* but **séver-al*[5]) and this fact requires the morphology to access metrical information about these forms.

One immediate benefit from the present analysis of the infix /ar/ in Sundancse is the ability to account for the unusual interaction between a nasal spread process and infixation. The nasal spread process in Sundanese is almost identical to the one already described in chapter 2 for Malay. The particular issue of interest is that /r/ normally blocks the spread of [nasal] onto following vowels. The data in (58) show the behavior of nasal spread and which segments act as blockers to this process.

(58) maro   [mǎro]   'to halve'
      maneh   [mǎněh]   'you'
      mandi   [mǎndi]   'to bath'
      niis   [nĩʔis]   'to take a holiday'
      miasih   [mĩǎsih]   'to love'

kumaha [kumãhã] 'how?'
ɲahoken [ɲãhõken] 'to inform'
bəŋhar [bəŋhằr] 'to be rich'

The data in (59) shows how infixation interacts with this nasalization process. The complicated aspect to this data is to explain how the vowels in (59) that occur after the infix receive nasalization.

(59) moekən [mõĕken] m-ar-oekən [mằroĕkən] 'to dry'
      ɲaur   [ɲăŭr]   ɲ-ar-aur   [ɲălaŭr]   'to say'
      niis   [nĭʔĭs]   n-ar-iis   [nằriʔĭs]   'to cool oneself'
      ɲaho   [ɲăhõ]   ɲ-ar-aho   [ɲằrahõ]   'to know'

If we consider the forms in (58), we see that non-nasal consonants[6] block nasal spread (cf. *mằrõ* not **mằrõ*, *mằndi* not **mằndĭ*, *mĭằsih* not **mĭằsĭh*). An additional opaque complexity to this pattern is a denasalization rule that denasalizes any vowel preceded by a non-nasal consonant (Anderson 1980:149). This rule denasalizes the vowels immediately following the infix /ar/ in (59). The question that remains is how do the vowels that follow these denasalized vowels receive their nasalization if the /r/ of the infix blocks nasal spread (we can also ask if /r/ blocks nasalization why is there a need for this denasalization rule).

The answer to these questions is readily apparent if we remember the analysis proposed for Malay nasal spread in section 2.2.1. The crucial part of that analysis is that all nasalized vowels in Malay are preceded by a [nasal] segment at sometime in the derivation. This characteristic is also true of the forms with infixes in (59) if we reconsider the phonological representation (57c). By simply allowing [nasal] to spread from left to right without requiring uniformity in this representation, we produce the post-nasalization representation in (60).

(60) $\# \rightarrow n \rightarrow \hat{\imath} \rightarrow ? \rightarrow \hat{\imath} \rightarrow s \rightarrow \%$
          $\downarrow \quad \uparrow$
          $\tilde{a} \rightarrow r$

The complex structure that has been built by the infix creates two different paths from the initial /n/ to all of the vowels in this form. Both the vowel of the infix and the vowels in the root are directly nasalized by /n/ because they are both preceded by /n/. This form can now be linearized, producing (61a), and then applying the denasalization rule to produce the correct form (61b).

(61)   a. $\# \rightarrow n \rightarrow \tilde{a} \rightarrow r \rightarrow \tilde{i} \rightarrow ? \rightarrow \tilde{i} \rightarrow s \rightarrow \%$
       b. $\# \rightarrow n \rightarrow \tilde{a} \rightarrow r \rightarrow i \rightarrow ? \rightarrow \tilde{i} \rightarrow s \rightarrow \%$

This completes an analysis of infixation of /ar/ in Sundanese. Both the placement of the affix and the complex interaction of it with a nasal spread process are directly accounted for by the precedence variables that are part of the phonological representation for this morpheme. The present analysis of nasal spread in Sundanese indicates that featural spread does not have to be local process in the surface form contra arguments made by Walker (1998b). The appearance of long distance spreading of nasality in Sundanese is an opacity effect where linearization and a denasalization rule obscure an earlier representation that nasalization operated on. Given the derivational approach in this model, the vowels that are nasalized in Sundanese are not local at the surface and do not share a single [nasal] feature.

The important insight into the behavior of infixes that is provided by the present proposals is that their unique behavior is due to there being two precedence variables in their phonological representation. Two precedence variables in a morpheme does not entail that it will be an infix though. Depending on what the temporal relationship between the two precedence relationships other surface effects are produced.

As discussed in chapter 2, reduplication results from a phonological representation that has a loop in it. Loops in a formative will be created whenever an affix is added where the beginning precedence variable specifies a point in the formative that is temporally later than the point specified by the ending precedence variable. To make this concrete, consider total reduplication in Indonesian. An example of this is *buku* 'book' which reduplicates as *buku-*

buku 'book (plural)'. The derivation for this form is presented in (62).

(62) a. *begin → end*   b. # → X ... X →%

    begin: __ → %
    end: # → __

    c. # → b → u → k → u → %

    d. # → b → u → k → u → %

(62a,b) gives the phonological representation of a precedence link that causes total reduplication. Since there is no segmental material added in conjunction with total reduplication, a precedence arrow directly links *begin* and *end*. Since there is no segmental material in this affix the only surface result is the repetition of the base that it is concatenated to.

This approach to reduplicative morphemes makes the implicit claim that reduplication is no different than the concatenation of any other morpheme. Depending on what types of precedence variables are contained in a given morpheme, different surface types of affixes (prefixes, suffixes, infixes, reduplication) are produced. Limiting the discussion to only reduplication, depending on what points in a formative are picked out by the precedence variables different patterns of reduplication can be created.

The total reduplication example in (62) appears to present the unmarked case for reduplication. Moravcsik (1978:328 fn. 13) indicates that total reduplication may be a true universal of human language since it appears that all languages have reduplication of some sort and that there is an implicational relationship between total reduplication and partial reduplication. If a language has a partial reduplication pattern then the language in question will also have total reduplication (Moravcsik 1978:328). These empirical facts coincide with the analytic unmarkedness of the precedence variables required to produce this pattern. The beginning and end of a formative are the two most prominent positions and this is supported by the commonness of prefixation and suffixation. Total reduplication utilizes the environments of both prefixation [# → __] and suffixation [__ → %] so there is a natural formal explanation for the frequency of this reduplication pattern.

Other reduplication patterns can be produced by making the environment specified by a precedence variable more complicated. This topic will be discussed in detail in section 3.4. The phonological specification of a morpheme that causes reduplication can be made more complicated in other ways. There is no reason not to allow segmental material to occur with loops. Just this situation obtains in phenomena referred to as prespecification or melodic overwriting in reduplication.

Alderete et al (1999) discusses the topic of prespecification in reduplication patterns in detail. They argue that Optimality Theory provides a deeper insight into this aspect of reduplication than previous approaches. To highlight their divergence from previous analyses of this type of reduplication data, Alderete et al use the term "fixed segmentism" instead of prespecification. One important aspect of Alderete et al's analysis that is correctly reflected by their change of terms is that they propose that there are actually two distinct sources of prespecification in reduplication patterns. They claim that one of the two types of sources for prespecification in reduplication is morphological in nature. This type of prespecification is evidenced in the reduplication patterns of Kamrupi (Alderete et al 1999:328) in (63a) and English *schm-* reduplication (Alderete et al 1999:355) in (63b).

(63) a. ghara   ghara-sara 'horse'/'horse and the like'
         khori   khori-sori 'fuel'/'fuel and the like'

      b. table-schmable
         resolutions-schmesolutions

Both reduplication patterns in (63) show the insertion of some segmental material in addition to reduplication. The Kamrupi example in (63a) shows the insertion of /s/ which appears to replace the onsets /gh/ and /kh/ respectively. The English examples show a similar behavior with /ʃm/ replacing the onset of each reduplicated word.

This type of prespecification in reduplication is morphological in nature for Alderete et al (1999) because there is no plausible way to derive the prespecified segments in a phonological approach from the emergence of the unmarked (McCarthy and Prince 1994a). Morphological prespecification always increases the markedness of a form in Alderete et al's eyes and since phonological alternations should always decrease the markedness of a form in some way within Optimality Theory this type of phenomenon cannot be phonological in nature.

While the model of reduplication developed here differs drastically in the assumptions made about the nature of phonology, an analysis similar in spirit to the one proposed by Alderete et al is available. To begin with, the presence of segmental material not present in the base is explained by positing this material as part of the phonological representation of the affix. The remainder of the analysis is simply to determining the precedence variables.

The examples in (63) only differ in the segmental content of the reduplicative affix. (64) and (65) show this by presenting what the phonological representation of the reduplicative affix is for Kamrupi and for English.

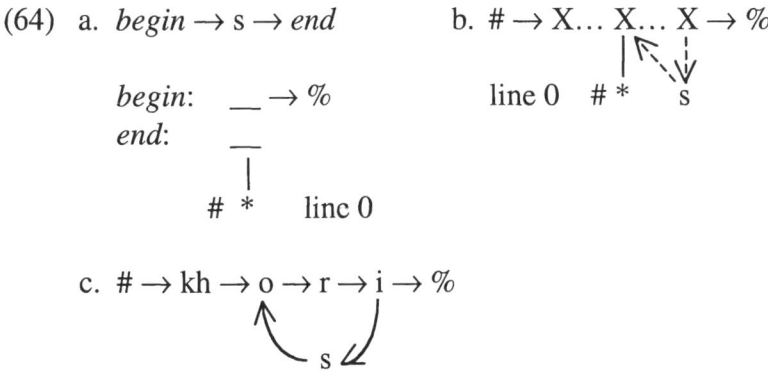

(64)   a. *begin* → s → *end*   b. # → X… X… X → %

    begin: __ → %   line 0   # *   s

    end: __

        # *   linc 0

   c. # → kh → o → r → i → %

          s

(65) a. *begin* → ∫ → m → *end*   b. # → X... X ... X → %

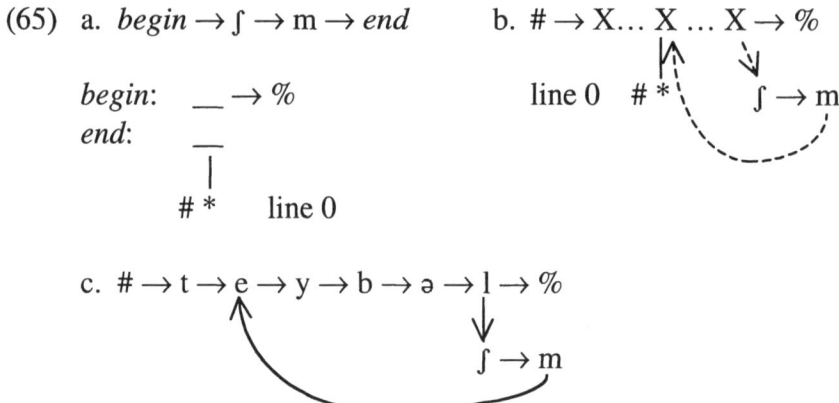

The precedence variables in (64a,b) and (65a,b) are the same as those used in analyses of infixation and suffixation. The precedence variable that specifies that an affix follows the end of the base is the *begin* precedence variable for this particular reduplication pattern. The *end* precedence variable is the environment that picks out the first vowel of a base as used in the Sundanese infixation example. There is nothing unusual in this type of reduplication pattern once the phonological representation of it is determined because it is constructed entirely of pieces we have already encountered.

Alderete et al (1999) argue that phonological cases of prespecification are inherently different from morphological ones. One of the cases of reduplication that Alderete et al present to illustrate this point is from Nancowry (Radhakrishnan 1981). A sampling of the data from this reduplication pattern in Nancowry is found in (66).

(66) cɯt   ʔit-cɯt   'to go, to come'
      rom   ʔum-rom   'flesh of fruit'/'to eat pandanus fruit'
      ɲiak   ʔuk-ɲiak   'binding'/'to bind'

The basic pattern of reduplication seen in (66) is the copying of the last segment of the base with a prespecified glottal stop onset and a prespecified high vowel that is either /i/ or /u/ prefixed to the base. This pattern will be discussed in greater detail in a moment.

Alderete et al's distinction between phonological and morphological cases of reduplication is based solely on Optimality Theory internal theoretical grounds. Simply, if the fixed segment is unmarked and can therefore be derived from an emergence of the unmarked (McCarthy and Prince 1994a) ranking of MAX_{IO} and MAX_{BR} then they declare that the pattern is phonological. Alderete et al argue that this is the case for the reduplication pattern in Nancowry in (66) since there is a reduction of the vowel inventory in the reduplicant and that reduplicants usually appear with a glottal stop in word initial position. According to Alderete et al's view, both of these surface effects are the result of miscopying with the goal of decreasing markedness in output forms (with /ʔ/ being the unmarked consonant and /i/ and /u/ being unmarked vowels).

However, Nancowry does not support this view of prespecification but to see why, we must first identify the issues at hand with respect to prespecification. There are four relevant questions: (1) do reduplication specific processes exist?, (2) is prespecification the result of morphology or phonology?, (3) what is the relationship between morphology and phonology?, and (4) which is a better approach to this phenomenon? invoking prespecification or cophonologies?

The answers to these questions that are implicit in Alderete et al's analyses are as follows. With regard to the first question, there *are* reduplication specific processes and this is a fundamental characteristic of the architecture of the correspondence theory approach to reduplication. Reduplication has its own correspondence relation (base/reduplicant correspondence) and there is also the abstract morpheme RED. This type of organization of the phonological grammar makes the claim that reduplication is unique and unlike other processes and that it requires its own correspondence relationship. The only way to avoid this situation is to pursue a RED-less model of reduplication within OT along the lines proposed by Raimy and Idsardi (1997). The empirical feasibility of this model is unclear due to a lack of work in this type of Optimality Theory grammar.

As already discussed, Alderete et al's response to the second question is that there are both cases of phonological and morphological prespecification. The phonological cases of prespecification that Alderete et al spend most of their time discussing are directly derivable from the emergence of the unmarked philosophy. Morphological prespecification is invoked in cases where the emergence of the unmarked approach will not work. This situation obtains when the prespecified segment is not the unmarked or default segment of the language, as in the English *schm-* reduplication. /ʃm/ is most definitely not the default onset type in English and thus a separate morpheme that introduces this segmental material into the forms is required.

The answer to the question about the relationship between morphology and phonology has also already been discussed. Optimality Theory assumes a non-modular relationship between morphology and phonology.

Finally, Alderete et al implicitly argue that cophonologies are preferable to prespecification in accounting for "fixed segmentism" effects. This position is indicated by the presentation of the emergence of the unmarked based analyses of prespecification phenomena where either a phonological or morphological approach are equally tenable. Alderete et al admit this analytic ambiguity but do not provide any explicit discussion of how it is to be resolved.

The most crucial difference in assumptions between Alderete et al and the analysis of Nancowry that will be developed here is about the relationship between morphology and phonology. As discussed earlier in this chapter, the model of reduplication being developed here assumes a modular relationship between morphology and phonology. According to this assumption, there is an independent level of representation where morphological structure is built. This morphological level precedes the phonology and provides the representations for the phonology to operate on. This organization allows for the morphology to construct phonological representations that must be altered in the phonology according to either language universal or language particular processes. Accordingly, non-surface true generalizations can be made at this morphological level that are then modified by the phonology.

Combining the assumption of a modular relationship between morphology and phonology with the analysis of reduplication presented so far, the other three assumptions about prespecification that differ from Alderete et al follow directly. Since we have identified the behavior of reduplicative affixes with the precedence variables there is no natural way to separate them from other affixes. All affixes require at least one precedence variable and all other differences result from what phonological material is stored for each affix. Consequently there is no natural way to distinguish between a reduplicative affix and other kinds of affixes except in a brute force way. This prevents reduplication from having any special characteristics or processes assessed to it in the phonology. The only way to create a reduplication specific effect is to stipulate that a particular affix (which happens to cause reduplication) behaves exceptionally in some manner. Additionally, since the difference between reduplicative affixes and non-reduplicative ones is based purely on the content of phonological material, it is equivalent to the difference between prefixes and suffixes or between affixes that have /i/ and affixes that have /t/ as segments in them. There is no special RED morpheme or other reduplication specific device. Following from these two points and the general architecture of the linguistic system assumed here, the morphological component should be the only source of prespecification.[7]

With the background assumptions in hand, we can now turn to the full set of data from Nancowry. Radhakrishnan (1981) is the primary source for data on Nancowry and (67) presents a representative sample of the data that Alderete et al (1999) analyze.

(67) a. (C)VC reduplicant
     ʔit-sút   'to rub'/'to kick with the foot'
     ʔin-ɲuán   'groaning noise'/'to groan'
     ʔit-các   'word'/'to pray'
     ʔin-séɲ   'to cut things to pieces'
     ʔup-kə́p   'to hold'/'to sting'
     ʔum-róm   'flesh of fruit'/'to eat pandanus fruit'
     ʔuk-ɲiák   'binding'/'to bind'
     ʔuŋ-míaŋ   'corner'

     b. (C)V reduplicant
     ʔi-tús   'to fall off (as a bird's feather)'/'to pluck out'
     ʔi-ruáy   'moving forward and backward'/'to beckon'

ʔu-ʔáw   'short barking noise'/'to bark'
ʔu-túaɬ   'round'/'a knot'

Note that (67) does not encompass all types of reduplicated forms. These additional forms will be added later when they become pertinent.

The main flaw in Alderete et al's analysis of Nancowry is the attribution of certain aspects of the reduplication pattern as resulting from reduplication specific phenomena. An adequate analysis should correctly identify which aspects of the reduplication pattern are due to general Nancowry phonology and which aspects result from the morphological specification of the reduplication morpheme.

The reduplication pattern that Radhakrishnan (1981) identifies in Nancowry has the following characteristics: the reduplicant is prefixed, the onset of the reduplicant is either /ʔ/ or Ø, the remainder of the reduplicant is either V or VC in shape, and the vowel is either /i/ or /u/. Of these four descriptive facts only the first one is uncontroversial. The remaining three are open to interpretation and discussion. The interpretation of these descriptive generalizations by Alderete et al does not reflect the best analysis of reduplication in Nancowry.

Alderete et al identify the miscopying of the onset of the root in Nancowry as a markedness reducing effect. This view of the presence of glottal stop in reduplicants is incorrect though. Radhakrishnan (1981:35) argues that there is a phonetic rule in Nancowry that inserts a glottal stop into all vowel initial syllables and this process explains the absence of onsetless syllables in Nancowry. Because of this independently motivated restriction on possible syllable types, we can analyze reduplication in Nancowry such that it does not copy the onset of the root. In support this claim, we can turn to a case where there is interaction between reduplication and further affixation.

In Nancowry there is an agentive morpheme /ma/ that alternates between /ma/ and /m/ depending on what kind of stem it is added to. For stems that are not reduplicated, this morpheme appears as /ma/ and when added to stems that are reduplicated it appears as

/m/. In addition to this alternation, reduplicated forms with the agentive morpheme do not have a glottal stop present in its onset. Radhakrishnan (1981:57-58) posits a sandhi rule that deletes both the vowel from /ma/ and the glottal stop from the reduplicated form in just this morphological circumstance. A simpler analysis is available though. If the glottal stop in reduplicants is the result of a phonetic epenthesis rule, reduplicants will be vowel initial at the point when /ma/ is added. Since onsetless syllables are banned in Nancowry, we can see the alternation in the agentive morpheme as the result of a hiatus rule that deletes /a/ when it is followed by another vowel. Consider the informal derivations in (68). The data is from Radhakrishnan (1981:57-58) although this author does not suggest the analysis presented in (68).

(68) Morphology   Phonology   Phonetics

     a. u-ʔɯ́ʔ   ⇒   u-ʔɯ́ʔ   ⇒   ʔu.ʔɯ́ʔ

     b. ma-u-ʔɯ́ʔ   ⇒   m-u-ʔɯ́ʔ   ⇒   mu.ʔɯ́ʔ

     c. ha-cím   ⇒   ha-cím   ⇒   ha.cím

     d. ma-ha-cím   ⇒   ma-ha-cím   ⇒   ma.ha.cím

In (68) we see morphological, phonological, and phonetic representations of four formatives. In (68a) reduplication is the only morphological process that has occurred. A vowel initial syllable is created by reduplication and later in the phonetics module a glottal stop is added to provide an onset. (68b) shows the addition of /ma/ in the morphology in addition to reduplication. In this case, the phonology is provided a sequence of two vowels and the /a/ is deleted. This representation then enters the phonetics and nothing needs to be done because there is no vowel initial syllable. (68c) and (68d) present cases where there is no onsetless syllable at any time in the derivation and thus no vowel deletion occurs in the phonology (the agentive /ma/ only occurs on unreduplicated stems if the causative morpheme /ha/ is present).

     Now that the glottal stop is identified as not being part of the reduplicant it should be noted that the actual templatic target for reduplication in Nancowry is a vowel initial syllable. This situation highlights the possibility of conflicting processes existing in separate modules. The morphological specification of reduplication in Nancowry specifies the reduplicant as a V(C) sequence even though a vowel initial syllable is not tolerated at the surface. If the morphology and phonology (and phonetics) are a single module, this type of conflict between morphological and phonological processes should not occur. Just such a situation is expected in a modular approach though.

Both Radhakrishnan (1981) and Alderete et al (1999) claim that whether a coda is copied in the reduplicant is a reduplication specific effect. Radhakrishnan (1981) posits the generalization that if the coda of the root is an oral or nasal stop the coda will be copied[8], otherwise the reduplicant will not have a coda. Alderete et al (1999:350-353) recast this generalization through the interaction of NoCODA and identity constraints that causes only non-continuants to copy as a coda. As argued by Alderete et al this is a kind of the emergence of the unmarked effect that claims that this restriction on codas is a reduplication specific effect.

A broader generalization about the distribution of codas in Nancowry is available if non-reduplicant syllables are considered. Radhakrishnan (1981:36) notes that not all the combinatorially possible heterosyllabic consonant clusters occur in his sample of Nancowry. A principled explanation of this gap in consonant clusters across syllables can be obtained if the interaction between stress and coda consonants is considered.

The dictionary of roots and derived forms included in Radhakrishnan (1981) indicates that unstressed syllables have a limited inventory of possible codas. The basic pattern is that all unstressed syllables pattern like reduplicants in that only oral and nasal stops are licensed.[9] There is a small amount of noise present in this generalization due to contradictions in Radhakrishnan (1981). In the dictionary section, there are four particles that are listed as unstressed which have continuants or glottal stops in their codas. In conflict with this is the list of particles (Radhakrishnan 1981:82) which contain these four items (*kuy* 'head', *cá?* 'face', *táy* 'hand' and *tow* no gloss given, but listed as a root with stress glossed 'heart' in the index of roots p.75). This list of particles states that they are actually roots. The issue of whether these morphemes are roots or not is important because Radhakrishnan (1981:15) states that all roots are stressed and in disyllabic roots the rightmost syllable receives stress. Since these apparent exceptions are actually roots, these particular morphemes support the generalization that only oral and nasal stops are permissible codas in unstressed syllables.

There are three marginal forms that are apparent counter examples to this generalization. The first is the form *ʔuʔ-ʔów* 'to vomit' which is a reduplicated form. This appears to be a truly exceptional form because it not only violates the proposed generalization about possible codas in unstressed syllables but it also violates Radhakrishnan's and Alderete et al's generalization that glottal stops should not copy in reduplication. Another exception is the form *kuɬmóre* 'gold' which is a borrowed word. Because it is a borrowed, we are unsure as to its actual morphological parse (Radhakrishnan does not provide one nor is this form listed in the root dictionary) so there is the possibility that the initial syllable has been analyzed as a root in Nancowry. The last remaining form is *caɬ-tǎc* 'frog' and it also does not have any morphological gloss provided. Due to the small number and lack morphological analysis of these exceptions it is clear that there is a generalization to be made about the distribution of codas in unstressed syllables in Nancowry.

The restriction of codas in unstressed syllables in Nancowry can be understood as a positional licensing or markedness effect (Hyman 1990, Beckman 1995, Zoll 1998) where the broader range of consonants is only licensed in onsets and stressed syllables. Accounting for this kind of phenomena does not distinguish between the analysis presented by Alderete et al and the modular analysis presented here so the formalization of this phenomenon will not be pursued further. The fact that the presence of a coda in a reduplicant can be predicted from non-reduplication specific information is an important fact that will be discussed when the modular approach is compared with Alderete et al (1999).

The remaining issue of the reduplication pattern in Nancowry is whether the vowel in the reduplicant is predictable or not. Alderete et al claim that the vowel is predictable but base their analysis on a small subset of reduplication data. Specifically, Alderete et al

(1999:139) limit their analysis to reduplicated forms that contain codas in the reduplicant or have a high glide, /ɬ/, or /s/ in the coda of the base. If a comprehensive sample of reduplicated forms in Nancowry is considered it is apparent that the vowel in the reduplicant is not predictable. Consider the data in (69).

(69) a. ʔu-ʔáw   'short barking noise'/'to bark'
         ʔi-sáw   'defecate'
         ʔu-túaɬ   'round'/'a knot'
         ʔi-ʔäɬ-a[10]   'twig'

     b. ʔu-yáʔ   'to leave something'/'to lay an egg'
         ʔi-náʔ-a   'handover something to some body'
         ʔu-ŋuáh   'erect'/'cliff'
         ʔi-kúah   'to shave'
         ʔu-téh   'to cut, to harvest'
         ʔi-tə́h   'to float'/'ignored'
         ʔu-ɲíh-a   'tree'
         ʔi-ɲíh   'to sell'

     c. ʔi-mũa   'twisted'/'to wring'
         ʔi-cí   'to decorate'
         ʔu-kɛ́   'to carry, to refill'

The forms in (69a) indicate that even in the selection of form types considered by Alderete et al (1999) vowel quality in the reduplicant is not predictable. (69a) shows near minimal pairs of roots ending in the high glide /w/ and /ɬ/ that show that whether the vowel in the reduplicant is /i/ or /u/ is an arbitrary fact of the root and not based on general phonological processes in Nancowry. The additional near minimal pairs in (69b,c) further reinforce the unpredictability and arbitrariness of vocalic quality in the reduplicant. When the entirety of the types of root forms and their reduplicants are considered, it is apparent that any analysis that claims the vowel in the reduplicant is predictable is untenable.

The distribution of vowels in reduplicants requires the setting up of an arbitrary distinction in the morphology where roots are marked as either /i/ roots or /u/ roots (similar in idea to theme vowels in Romance languages). This approach is necessary and sufficient to account for all of the reduplicated forms in Nancowry. While the partial regularity of some reduplicated forms that Alderete et al use as the basis for their analysis tempt one to posit a phonological generalization, this move is neither sufficient nor necessary to account for the entire data set. Thus, the claim that the vowel in reduplicants in Nancowry is predictable should be abandoned.

Now that the pertinent generalizations in Nancowry have been identified, the phonological representation of the reduplicative affix can be identified. To obtain the particular pattern of reduplication in Nancowry, a precedence variable occurs in the "middle" of other phonological material and this variable will be referred to as *middle*. This simple modification will allow the reduplication pattern in Nancowry to be presented.[11]

(70) a. $\# \rightarrow i/u \rightarrow middle \rightarrow end$ b. $\# \rightarrow \{i,u\}$

$$middle \; \underline{\quad} \rightarrow \%$$
$$end \quad \# \rightarrow \underline{\quad}$$

$$\# \rightarrow X \; \dots \; X \rightarrow \%$$

The discontinuous nature of the reduplication pattern in Nancowry is captured by (70a,b) through the presence of a "middle" precedence variable. Informally (70a,b) states, "/i/ or /u/ precede the last segment of the base which precedes the first segment of the base". Each root will be classified as either an /i/ root or an /u/ root and this will determine whether an /i/ or /u/ appears in the reduplicant. The use of a "middle" precedence variable to produce discontinuous reduplication patterns is supported by analyses of Temiar and Semai that are presented in section 3.4.5.

We can now turn to example derivations that show how the reduplication patterns in Nancowry are produced by the phonological specification of the affix in (70) and general phonological processes in Nancowry. No reduplication specific behavior is present in this analysis. Note that the morphology spells out phonological material in a cyclic fashion starting with the base and moving outward.

(71) ʔu-ŋuáh 'erect'/'cliff'

Morphology = [affix ^{U}[ŋuáh]]
spell-out base   *spell-out affix*

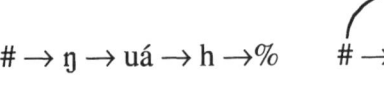

→ ŋ → uá → h →%   # → ŋ → uá → h → %

Phonology   Phonetics
linearize   *coda licensing*   *glottal stop epenthesis*
uh-ŋuáh   u-ŋuáh   ʔu-ŋuáh

(72) ʔi-tús   'to fall off [bird's feather]'/'to pluck out'

Morphology = [affix ^{I}[tus]]
spell-out base   *spell-out affix*

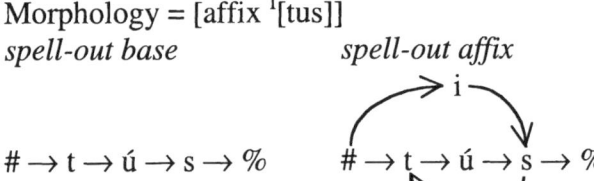

→ t → ú → s → %   # → t → ú → s → %

Phonology   Phonetics
linearize   *coda licensing*   *glottal stop epenthesis*
is-tús   i-tús   ʔi-tús

(73) ʔi-cí   'to decorate'

Morphology = [affix ^{I}[cí]]
spell-out base   *spell-out red*

→ c → í → %   # → c → í → %

Phonology   Phonetics
linearize   *coda licensing*   *glottal stop epenthesis*
ií-cí   i-cí   ʔi-cí

The three derivations in (71-73) all follow a similar path. Cyclic spell out in the morphological component begins by exchanging the morpho-syntactic features of the base for the corresponding phonological representation (spell-out base). After this, the phonological content of the reduplicative morpheme is then spelled-out. This completes the spell-out in the morphological component. The representation is then passed onto the phonology where phonological rules have an opportunity to apply. Due to our specific interest in reduplication in Nancowry, the next step of the deriva- tion consists of linearizing the phonological representation. After linearization, the coda licensing rule applies which will delete any continuant or glottal segments in a coda in an unstressed syllable. Finally, the phonological representation is passed to the phonetics module where a glottal stop is added to the vowel initial syllable and the surface form results.

The different forms in (71-73) were chosen to demonstrate the different characteristics of Nancowry reduplication. (71) and (72) contrast in what vowel they take in the reduplicant which is indi- cated by the superscript /i/ or /u/ on the base. Whether a root takes an /i/ or /u/ is an arbitrary lexical fact. All three forms show some sort of simplification of the reduplicant because it is an unstressed syllable. (71) deletes /h/ from its coda in the reduplicant and (72) does the same to /s/. (73) shows that the coda licensing rule should probably be extended to a general unstressed syllable licensing rule that will also reduce vowel sequences in these metrical positions. Radhakrishnan (1981) indicates that there is a reduced inventory of vowels in unstressed syllables. Only simplex vowels /i/, /u/ or /a/ appear in unstressed syllables so the stress system will also provide the information to reduce the long vowel /ii/ in (73) to simplex /i/.

The other types of roots in Nancowry that have an oral or nasal stop in coda position will be derived in the same fashion as the ex- amples in (71-73). The only difference is that the coda in the redu- plicant will not be deleted by the coda licensing rule. The analysis presented will account for all of the reduplicated forms present in Radhakrishnan. The exceptional forms previously mentioned with /ʔ/ and /ɬ/ in coda position can also be accommodated in this analy- sis through the use of an exception mark (Chomsky and Halle 1968) which would prevent these codas from being deleted by the coda licensing rule.

We first compare the two analyses of Nancowry on empirical coverage. The analysis presented here is clearly superior because it accommodates all of the known reduplication data in Nancowry. The analysis in Alderete et al (1999) only accounts for a subset of this data. Further comparisons can only be made once the Alderete et al analysis is revised to account for the full range of facts.

To begin the modification of the Alderete et al analysis it must be noted that there is one aspect of the model of reduplication assumed by Alderete et al than cannot be modified. This aspect of Alderete et al's model of reduplication is pathological overgeneration. This overgeneration is due to the typological claims made by Alderete et al. The typological claim (Alderete et al 1999:333) relevant to this point is found in (74).

(74) *Reduplication/Inventory relation III*:
      Any phonological restriction on the reduplicant of one language is a possible restriction on the whole of another language.

The importance of this claim is what it implies for Alderete et al's analysis of the Nancowry form *ʔi-tús* 'to pluck out' (from *tús* 'to fall off [as a bird's feather]'). Alderete et al claim that the /s/ maps to /i/ in the reduplicant as a result of the high ranking of R-ANCHOR$_{BR}$ and the coda condition they posit to force this alternation. This aspect of their analysis when taken in light of the typological claim in (74) leads to the prediction that we should find languages that map /s/ to /i/ in their non-reduplicative phonology. This is a false prediction. No known language has this mapping. Modifying the particular Optimality Theory analysis of Nancowry does not remove this overgeneration aspect of the correspondence theory of reduplication because the analysis presented in Alderete et al (1999) is a plausible analysis and there is no apparent theoretical reason to rule out this particular constraint ranking. It appears that pathological overgeneration is an inherent property of the model of reduplication espoused by Alderete et al.

The first modification to Alderete et al's analysis must be to adopt a melodic overwriting approach to the vowels in the reduplicant. Roots will be assigned to either /i/ or /u/ classes which will account for what vowel appears in the reduplicant. The prefixal nature of this vowel can be captured through a relatively high ranked alignment constraint stating that this morpheme needs to be at the left edge of a formative. The appearance of the epenthetic glottal stop can be accounted for by ranking ONSET above this generalized alignment constraint so this morpheme will be minimally displaced from the left edge of the word by a glottal stop in order to satisfy ONSET. The interaction with the agentive /ma/ morpheme will result by ranking the generalized alignment constraint that requires /ma/ to be a prefix above the generalized alignment constraint requiring the vowel in the reduplicant to be a prefix. (75) presents a tableau that shows this interaction.

(75)

ma, u, ʔúi̯ʔ	ONSET	ALIGN(ma, L)	ALIGN(u, L)
a. ma.u.ʔúi̯ʔ	*!		**
☞ b. mu.ʔúi̯ʔ			*
c. ʔa.mu.ʔúi̯ʔ		*!*	
d. ma.ʔu.ʔúi̯ʔ			**!*

If the generalized alignment constraints that require both affixes to be at the left are evaluated by how many segments are between the left edge of an affix and the left edge of a word, then the interaction between ONSET, ALIGN(ma, L) which requires the affix /ma/ to be a prefix, and ALIGN(u, L) which requires the prespecified vowel to be a prefix accounts for the deletion of the vowel in /ma/. ONSET in Nancowry will be undominated since no surface forms provide any evidence to demote this constraint. ALIGN(ma, L) is ranked above ALIGN(u, L) because /ma/ occurs to the left of /u/ in forms that have both of these affixes. The most harmonic candidate given this particular constraint ranking is (75b). This candidate has deleted the /a/ from /ma/ which allows all syllables to have onsets and moves the affix /u/ one segment closer to the left edge. Candidate (75a) violates ONSET. Candidate (72c) places /u/ to the left of /ma/ causing violations of ALIGN(ma, L). Finally, candidate (75d) shows that simply inserting a glottal stop to satisfy ONSET is not optimal because it displaces /u/ farther away from the left edge of the word.

Accounting for the presence of the coda consonant in the reduplicant can be handled by ranking constraints that ensure RED is present in the output below the coda condition on unstressed syllables that is required for the overall phonology of Nancowry. This move has an interesting effect though because it basically mimics an allomorphy based account of the presence of the coda in the reduplicant. RED as a morpheme will only have phonetic realization when the coda that can be copied does not violate the coda condition on unstressed syllables. Following proposals made by Walker (1998a) on the morphological make up of prespecified reduplication patterns, there are two distinct morphemes in the Nancowry reduplication pattern. One morpheme supplies the prespecified /i/ or /u/ and another separate morpheme is RED. Thus, output forms with only the prespecified vowel will violate REALIZE(RED) while reduplicants that have reduplicated a coda will not. The tableaux in (76) and (77) show the interaction of the CODA CONDITION and REALIZE(RED).

(76)

i, RED, tus	R-ANC	CODA COND	REAL(RED)	*STRUCT	MAX$_{BR}$
a. ?is.tus		*!		*****	**
☞ b. ?i.tus			*	*****	***
c. ?i.tus.tus		*!		********	
d. ?it.tus	*!			*****	**

(77)

u, RED, rom	R-ANC	CODA COND	REAL(RED)	*STRUCT	MAX$_{BR}$
☞ a. ?um.rom				*****	**
b. ?u.rom			*!	*****	***
c. ?u.rom.rom				*******!*	
d. ?ur.rom	*!	*		*****	**

R-ANC is the R-ANCHOR$_{BR}$ constraint proposed by Alderete et al (1999:349) that captures the generalization that the coda of the base is copied. CODA COND is a cover constraint that encompasses the generalization that unstressed coda are restricted to oral and nasal stops. REAL(RED) ensures that there is some segmental exponence of the RED morpheme in the output. *STRUCT penalizes each segment present in the output and MAX$_{BR}$ is the correspondence constraint that penalizes incomplete copying of the base.

The constraint ranking in both (76) and (77) shows that both R-ANC and CODA COND dominate REAL(RED) indicating that no copying should occur if a licit coda in the base is not available. REAL(RED) dominates *STRUCT otherwise there would be no reduplication present in the surface forms at all. Finally, *STRUCT dominates MAX$_{BR}$ and this limits reduplication when it occurs to a single segment.

(76) shows that when the coda of the base violates CODA COND, no reduplication occurs as in the winning candidate (76b). Attempting to copy a different consonant from the base violates R-ANC as seen in candidate (76d). Candidate (76c) shows that copying more than a single consonant only adds violations of *STRUCT without satisfying other higher ranked constraints.

(77) shows that when the coda of the base does not violate CODA COND then the most harmonic candidate is one that copies only the coda of the base as shown in candidate (77a). Non-copying of the coda leads to a violation of REAL(RED) as in candidate (77b). Additional copying of consonants as in candidate (77c) adds gratuitous violations of *STRUCT and (77d) shows that copying the onset of the base causes violation of R-ANC.

The required modifications to the Alderete et al analysis raise the question of whether this phonological analysis of the reduplicant in Nancowry will be favored by a learner over a pure allomorphy analysis where roots are classified into two classes one of which also has RED (ones that have codas in their reduplicants) and one where only the vowel is an exponent of the morphology. This "allomorphy problem" results directly from the pursuit of a parallel analysis of reduplication. Optimality Theory does not necessarily require a fully parallel architecture (Prince and Smolensky 1993, McCarthy 1999, Kiparsky 1998, Ito and Mester 1999) and chapter 2 shows that the argument for parallelism in reduplication based on backcopying effects (McCarthy and Prince 1995) is no longer valid. So another possible modification to the Alderete et al analysis is to adopt a certain amount of derivation and allow an intermediate calculation in Nancowry where all codas copy into the reduplicant. This strengthens the claim made by Alderete et al (1999) that R-ANCHOR$_{BR}$ plays a defining role in spelling out the reduplicant in Nancowry. To finish this sketch of a derivational Optimality Theory analysis of Nancowry is to place the unstressed coda restriction into the second strata of constraints and this will then remove all illicit codas in unstressed syllables and produce the correct surface forms. The main benefit of this derivational Optimality Theory analysis is that there is no issue of allomorphy in the appearance of RED in the output.

The Alderete et al analysis of Nancowry has been modified to incorporate the correct generalizations about Nancowry phonology and the result of these modifications is an Optimality Theory analysis that does not support *any* of the major claims put forth by Alderete et al (1999). The emergence of the unmarked aspects of Nancowry reduplication as argued for by Alderete et al (1999) must be abandoned if the vowel quality and appearance of the glottal stop at the surface is accounted for in all of the data. The analysis of the presence of the coda in the reduplicant also must abandon the emergence of the unmarked approach because it can be predicted from the general phonology of Nancowry. The parallelism aspect of Alderete et al's analysis could be saved but only at the cost of the adoption of an allomorphy based analysis of reduplication in Nancowry. Alternatively, the allomorphy issue can be eliminated by abandoning a parallel analysis and adopting a derivational model of Optimality Theory.

The modified Optimality Theory analysis that emerges from Alderete et al (1999) is a pale replica of the modular analysis presented here. Both analyses account for the data but they are not equivalent in how the generalizations are captured. The modular analysis captures deep regularities in the morphology and phonology of Nancowry with simple rules. The simplicity of the rules and broadness of the generalizations made are a direct result of the multiple levels of representation (and consequent opacities) that are present in a modular approach. Word formation regularities can be separated from phonological rules that obscure the correct generalizations. All of these results are due to the general architecture of classical generative phonology (Chomsky and Halle 1968, Leben 1973, Goldsmith 1976). Optimality Theory in general is a response to and denial of the claims made by classical generative phonology about the nature of phonology. Nancowry provides an explicit case where in order for Optimality Theory to account for the complete set of data it must recapitulate most of the assumptions and architecture of classical generative phonology into an Optimality Theory grammar. This should raise serious questions about the nature of the arguments in favor of Optimality Theory.

Returning to the main topic of this section, the analyses of pre-specification effects in reduplication and infixation presented here indicate that the difference between prefixes and suffixes and other non-concatenative affixes is not that great. Differences among affix types directly result from the phonological material that is associated with a morpheme. From this point the behavior of prefixes, suffixes, infixes, and reduplication can be derived from the same pool of resources and this is a major advance in the understanding of affixation. This result cashes in on the claim made by Marantz (1982) that reduplication is just a type of affixation and requires no special mechanisms. The only aspect of the analysis of reduplication presented here that could possibly be interpreted as reduplication specific is the linearization process in the phonology. Taking this view of linearization misunderstands the motivation for this process though. Linearization of phonological representations so that they are interpretable by the phonetics or the motor control interface is a requirement for all models of phonology. The fact that reduplication appears to be the only morphological construction that shows overt effects of the linearization process does not in any way support the idea that linearization is reduplication specific. This view is also wrong.

The analysis of infixation in Sundanese shows that infixation can also produce opaque interactions due to the complex precedence structure that results from the concatenation of an infix. Also, new insights into geminate inalterability effects (Schein and Steriade 1986) might be provided given the phonological representations proposed in chapter 2. Because of the inherent multiple environ-

ments of a single melody in a geminate structure, the Uniformity
Parameter is a natural candidate to encode whether a process will
show geminate inalterability or not. The analysis of morphological
gemination in Chaha in chapter 2 shows that using self-loops to describe gemination is useful in understanding how geminate structures can interact with phonological rules. From these examples we
can see that the complex representations proposed to account for
reduplication have immediate and beneficial repercussions on other
types of nonconcatenative morphology.

3.4   Deriving reduplicative templates

One of the goals of any model of reduplication should be to provide
an explanation of the possible surface patterns of reduplication. Research into this topic is best represented by Prosodic Morphology
(McCarthy and Prince 1986) and recent Optimality Theory work
(McCarthy and Prince 1994a, 1994b, Urbanczyk 1996, Spaelti 1997
and others). All of this work shares in common the assumption that
reduplication patterns are the result of surface output goals that pre-
scribe some sort of prosodic target. Early work in Prosodic Morphology (McCarthy and Prince 1986, 1993b, 1994a) described
these surface outputs through the use of prosodic templates that
specified the surface target. Later work (McCarthy and Prince
1994b, Urbanczyk 1996, Spaelti 1997) has attempted to derive
these surface templates through the interaction of constraints with a
certain amount of success.

The main problem with this approach to reduplicative templates
is that it denies the lexical aspect of reduplication. There is a necessary level of stipulation present in all reduplicative templates because it is a lexical fact of any given morpheme what the pattern of
reduplication should be. The existence of languages that show multiple distinct patterns of reduplication argue strongly for this point.
Thus in practice there are many different reduplicative morphemes
(RED_1, RED_2, RED_3, etc.) each inducing their own base reduplicant
faithfulness constraints (McCarthy and Prince 1995:265). If a reduplication pattern is only and truly a derivative of language specific

features then there should be no possibility of multiple patterns of reduplication in a single language. A second problem with the attempt to derive reduplicative templates from the interaction of constraints is that this approach denies the generalization that is encompassed by the phonological content of a morpheme. The Optimality Theory approach that claims that RED has no phonological content and then derives the surface phonology of the reduplicative morpheme through the interaction of constraints denies the morphological nature of the affix in question.

The approach to reduplicative templates that will be presented here derives the surface forms of reduplicative affixes directly from their phonological representation. Depending on what precedence variables are present in an affix different surface realizations occur. In this approach there is no output goal, only the underlying precedence variables that are part of the phonological representation of the reduplicative morpheme. A benefit of this approach is that a typology of markedness of templates can be derived through analytic simplicity. To see how this aspect of this approach to reduplicative templates is achieved consider the reduplication patterns in the following sections.

3.4.1 Total reduplication

As discussed earlier, total reduplication is the least marked reduplication pattern that occurs in natural languages and may be a true language universal (Moravcsik 1978:328). This unmarked status is indicated by the representation in (78) for a precedence link that causes total reduplication.

(78) a. *begin* → *end*   b.
$$\# \to X \dots X \to \%$$

      begin: __ → %
      end: # → __

The precedence relationship specified in (78) is that the last segment of a precedence graph precedes the first segment. This creates a loop in the phonological representation where all the segments are part of the loop. Consequently, total reduplication results when the formative is linearized.

Reconsider the data from Malay discussed in chapter 2. (79) presents this pattern of total reduplication in Malay.

(79) hamã̄   'germ'   hămã̄-hămã̄   'germs'
      waŋ̃ĩ   'fragrant'   wăŋ̃ĩ-wăŋ̃ĩ   'fragrant (intens.)'
      aŋăn   'reverie'   ăŋăn-ăŋăn   'ambition'
      aŋĕn   'wind'   ăŋĕn-ăŋĕn   'unconfirmed news'

Although all the forms in (79) show total reduplication it is not clear what semantic change each of the forms have in common. This fact supports the position that reduplication results from a re-adjustment rule and we can set aside for the present analysis what the content of the morpho-syntactic or semantic feature is triggering total reduplication in Malay. The important part is that the redupli-cated forms in Malay are morphologically complex in that they have a morpho-syntactic representation such as in (80). This repre-sentation simply indicates that there is some sort of affix attached to the root which triggers a readjustment rule (as indicated by the [+RR] feature).

(80)

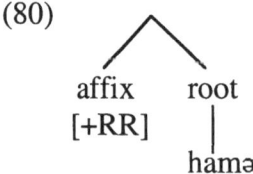

The affix in (80) is a zero morph phonologically, but it does trigger the readjustment rule that adds a precedence link of the form in (78). Consider the spell-out derivation of (80) in (81).

(81) a. $\# \rightarrow h \rightarrow a \rightarrow m \rightarrow \partial \rightarrow \%$

      b. $\# \rightarrow h \rightarrow a \rightarrow m \rightarrow \partial \rightarrow \%$

(81a) shows the result of spelling-out the root morpheme in (80). The Ilokano example presented earlier in this chapter indicated that a readjustment rule applies before the morpheme that triggers it is spelled out and this results in (81b). The affix is then spelled-out as a zero morph and this does not change (81b).

An important aspect of this approach to total reduplication is that the beginning and end of a precedence structure is determined by what phonological material has been spelled-out at the point in the derivation where the reduplicative loop is added. Consequently, depending on the morphological scope of affixes different combinations of roots and affixes can be reduplicated as part of total reduplication. Indonesian (Uhrbach 1987, McCarthy and Prince 1995:334-335) presents a case of total reduplication that shows just this type of scope effect. Depending on the scope of the affixes involved, the prefix /məN/ will either appear before the stem that is reduplicated or in-between the stem and its reduplicant. In neither pattern is this prefix reduplicated. Consider the data in (82).

(82) a. potoŋ   'cut'   pukul   'hit'
         tulis   'write'   hormat   'respect'
         tari   'dance'   isi   'contents'

     b. mə-motoŋ-motoŋ   'to cut (intensive/repetitive)'
         mə-nulis-nulis   'to write (intensive/repetitive)'
         mə-nari-nari   'to dance (intensive/repetitive)'
         məŋ-isi-isi   'to fill with various things'

     c. pukul-məm-ukul   'to hit (reciprocal)'
         tari-mən-ari   'to dance (reciprocal)'
         hormat-meŋ-hormat-i   'to respect (reciprocal)'

The forms in (82a) show the stems without any affixation. (82b) shows forms where /məN/, which is an "active" marker on verbs, appears as a prefix to the reduplicated root along with overapplication of a nasal substitution process. (82c) shows forms that have /məN/ interposed between the copies of the root with normal application of the nasal assimilation process. Capturing the behavior of the nasal substitution process is a crucial aspect in explaining this pattern of total reduplication.

Both the difference between placement of /məN/ and reduplicant and the behavior of the nasal substitution rule can be derived through the order in which morphemes are concatenated once the nature of the nasal substitution process is understood. The approach that will be developed assumes that the morphemes for intensive/repetitive and reciprocal are distinct morphemes that have different scope relations with respect to /məN/. Both of these morphemes trigger a readjustment rule that causes total reduplication. Before we explore this point further, we must establish what the formal nature of nasal substitution in Indonesian is given the precedence representations used in this book.

Uhrbach (1987) argues that the substitution in Indonesian is in essence a two-part process. The first part is the spreading of place features onto the nasal segment in /məN/ which does not have place features of its own. Uhrbach claims that this process results from a universal rule of feature spreading that provides place features to segments without them. The second part of the nasal substitution process is the "deletion" of a voiceless stop that follows the nasal segment in /məN/. Consider the data[12] in (83) from Uhrbach (1987:73).

(83) pilih   məmilih   '(to) choose'
      bəli   məmbəli   '(to) buy'
      tipu   mənipu   '(to) trick someone'
      doroŋ   məndoroŋ   '(to) push'
      kotor   məŋotor   '(to) soil something'
      goreŋ   məŋgoreŋ   '(to) fry something'
      isi   məɲisi   'contents/to fill'

The issue that must be determined with respect to the "deletion" of the voiceless segments in (83) is whether this deletion is the result of a "jump link" or of the coalescence of the nasal and following voiceless segment.

The overapplication facts in (82b) indicate that there must be a coalescence rule operating in these forms. This rule will coalesce the nasal and following voiceless segment into a single segment as discussed in the Chumash example in section 2.2.2. This rule can be formulated as in (84).

(84)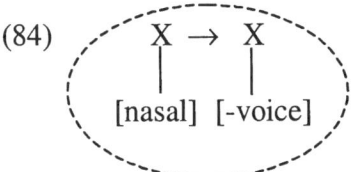

The process in (84) removes the precedence information between the two specified segments and combines these segments into a single segment that retains all other precedence relations. (85) presents an example derivation showing the application of both the nasal assimilation rule and the coalescence rule.

(85) a. $\# \rightarrow p \rightarrow o \rightarrow t \rightarrow o \rightarrow \eta \rightarrow \%$

  $m \rightarrow \partial \rightarrow N$

  b. $\# \rightarrow p \rightarrow o \rightarrow t \rightarrow o \rightarrow \eta \rightarrow \%$

  $m \rightarrow \partial \rightarrow m$

  c. $\# \rightarrow p \rightarrow o \rightarrow t \rightarrow o \rightarrow \eta \rightarrow \%$

  $m \rightarrow \partial \rightarrow m$

  d. $\# \rightarrow m \rightarrow o \rightarrow t \rightarrow o \rightarrow \eta \rightarrow \%$

  $m \rightarrow \partial$

(85a) shows the representation that is given to the phonology by the morphology. (85b) shows the result of the spreading of the place features from the voiceless consonant to the nasal segment. (85c) shows that the environment for the coalescence rule is met and (85d) shows the resulting coalesced segment and precedence graph. A Derived Environment Condition must be placed on this coales-

cence rule since there are sequences of a nasal segment preceding a
voiceless segment in monomorphemic words in Indonesian[13] (e.g.
məmaləmkan 'to stay overnight', *maŋsai* 'tangled').

Given the coalescence view of nasal substitution we can now
account for the preposed forms in (82b) that show overapplication
of this process. First, the morphological structure of these forms
must be discussed. Since, /məN/ does not reduplicate in these particular forms we can assume that /məN/ has scope over the inten-
sive/repetitive morpheme. This relationship produces the morpho-
syntactic structure in (86).

(86)

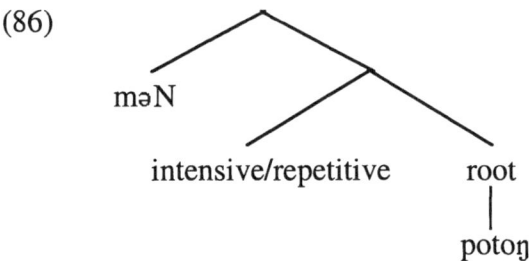

məN

intensive/repetitive   root

                             |
                             potoŋ

The morpho-syntactic structure in (86) produces the spell-out of
phonological material seen in (87). Note that the intensive/receptive
morpheme is a zero morph that triggers a readjustment rule which
causes total reduplication.

(87)   a. $\# \rightarrow p \rightarrow o \rightarrow t \rightarrow o \rightarrow \eta \rightarrow \%$

       b. $\# \rightarrow p \rightarrow o \rightarrow t \rightarrow o \rightarrow \eta \rightarrow \%$

       c. $\# \rightarrow p \rightarrow o \rightarrow t \rightarrow o \rightarrow \eta \rightarrow \%$
          $m \rightarrow ə \rightarrow N$

(87a) shows the spell-out of the root. (87b) shows the application of
the readjustment rule triggered by the intensive/repetitive morpheme. Since this morpheme is phonologically null, no other

phonological material is added. Finally, (87c) shows the spell-out and concatenation of /məN/.

(87c) is the representation that the phonology receives. This representation undergoes the derivation in (88).

(88) a.
$$\# \to p \to o \to t \to o \to \eta \to \%$$
$$m \to \vartheta \to m$$

b.
$$\# \to p \to o \to t \to o \to \eta \to \%$$
$$m \to \vartheta \to m$$

c.
$$\# \to m \to o \to t \to o \to \eta \to \%$$
$$m \to \vartheta$$

d. $\# \to m \to \vartheta \to m \to o \to t \to o \to \eta \to m \to o \to t \to o \to \eta \to \%$

(88a) shows the spreading of the place features from the segment that follows the nasal segment. (88b) shows the environment for the coalescence rule and (88c) shows the resulting precedence structure. (88c) is then linearized which produces (88d) a form that shows overapplication of nasal substitution. As before, overapplication in this case results from a rule that applies before linearization occurs. Forms that do not undergo nasal substitution are also accounted for since their representations will be equivalent to (88a) with respect to the precedence graph. Since the loop created by the reduplication readjustment rule does not include the nasal segment from /məN/, this segment will not be repeated by the linearization process.

Now that the preposed forms in (82b) have been accounted for we must focus on the interposed forms in (82c). These forms have /məN/ occurring between the two copies of the stem and do not show overapplication of nasal substitution. The main source of this different behavior is due to the morpho-syntactic structure of these forms. The relationship between the reciprocal affix and /məN/ is that the reciprocal affix has scope over /məN/. This produces the morpho-syntactic structure in (89).

(89)

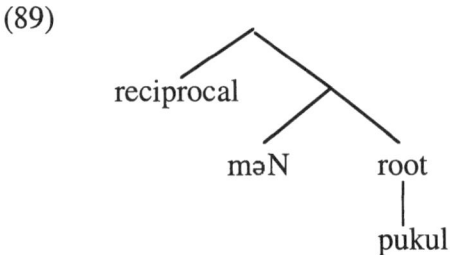

The difference in morpho-syntactic structure between (89) and (86) causes a different precedence structure to be created for forms with the morpho-syntactic structure of (89) as opposed to the precedence structure for preposed forms in (87). Given the ordering of affixation in (89) and the phonological specification of total reduplication the representations in (90) are built by the morphology.

(90) a. $\# \rightarrow p \rightarrow u \rightarrow k \rightarrow u \rightarrow l \rightarrow \%$

b. $\# \rightarrow p \rightarrow u \rightarrow k \rightarrow u \rightarrow l \rightarrow \%$
$\qquad m \rightarrow \partial \rightarrow N$

c. $\# \rightarrow p \rightarrow u \rightarrow k \rightarrow u \rightarrow l \rightarrow \%$
$\qquad m \rightarrow \partial \rightarrow N$

(90a) shows the spell-out of the root. (90b) shows the concatenation of /məN/ with the root and (90c) then shows the result of the readjustment rule triggered by the reciprocal morpheme. The last segment in (90b) is definitely the /l/ and the first segment is /m/ instead of /p/ since /məN/ was added later in the morphological derivation.

The precedence graph in (90c) must produce a linearized form that does not show overapplication of the nasal substitution and this fact indicates that that coalescence rule in (84) will not help in explaining the behavior of the interposed forms. If the coalescence rule were to apply to (90c) the following derivation would occur.

(91)   a. # → p → u → k → u → l → %

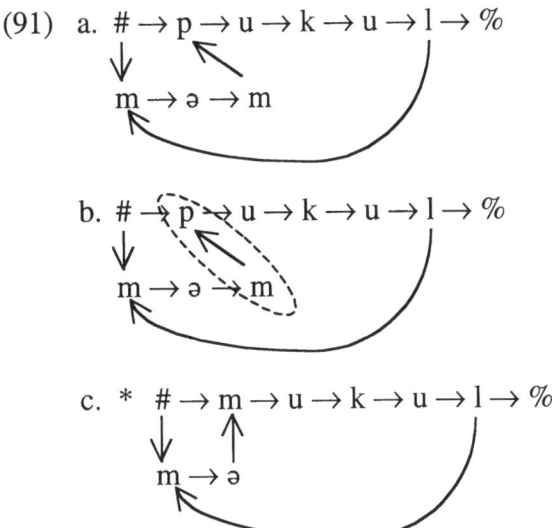

b. # → p → u → k → u → l → %

c. * # → m → u → k → u → l → %

The representation in (91c) is the result of the application of feature spreading to give the placeless nasal place features, (91a), and the application of the coalescence rule in (91b). It is obvious that (91c) can not produce the correct interposed form, *pukul-mə-mukul*, since there is no /p/ segment present in (91c).

There is another possible interpretation of the nasal substitution process where "deletion" of the voiceless segment following the nasal segment results from a jump link. This interpretation of this aspect of the nasal substitution process would be instantiated by the rule in (92).

(92)

$$X \;\to\; X \;\to\; X$$
$$| \qquad\quad |$$
$$\text{[nasal]} \quad \text{[-voice]}$$

The rule in (92) indicates that when a nasal segment is followed by a voiceless segment a link from the nasal segment to the segment that follows the voiceless segment is added. This rule requires a Derived Environment Condition to be met, just as the coalescence rule in (84) did, to ensure that it does not apply in monomorphemic forms.

Given the rule in (91), a different phonological derivation for the morphological representation in (90c) can be given. Consider the derivation in (93).

(93)

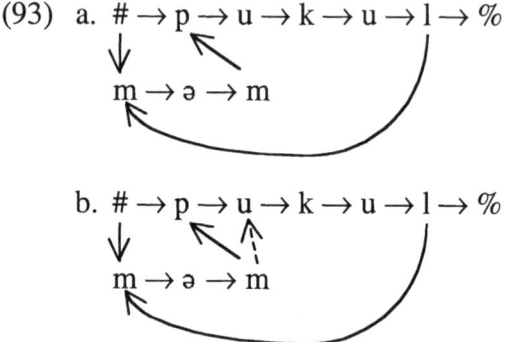

(93b) shows the phonological representation that results from the nasal segment receiving place features in (93a) and the application of the rule in (91) that adds the link from the /m/ in the prefix to the /u/ of the stem.

The linearization of (93b) calls attention to the optimization aspects of linearization. Because of the back loop links to the prefix /məN/ there is more than a single way to linearize the precedence graph in (93b). The presence of the added jump link from the end of /məN/ to /u/ in the root is another crucial complicating factor. Linearization of the precedence graph in (93b) shows the interaction of different principles of the linearization process.

The interposed position of /məN/ results from the principle of using the most recently added information first and the optimization aspect of linearization. According to the morphological structure of the interposed forms presented in (89), the back link added by the reciprocal morpheme has a greater importance than the /məN/ morpheme. The linearization algorithm will be driven to pursue a linearization that utilizes the higher priority links as soon as possible. This particular goal will cause the interposition of /məN/ given a morphological structure as in (89). To show this, consider an interposed form that does not show nasal substitution. *hormat-meŋ-hormat-i* 'to respect (reciprocal)' is this kind of form and (94) presents its phonological derivation.

(94) a.

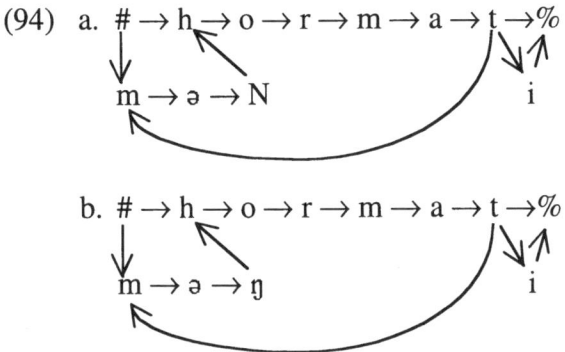

    c. hormat-məŋ-hormat-i
    d. *məŋ-hormat-məŋ-hormat-i
    e. *məŋ-hormat-i

(94a) presents the phonological representation created by the morphology and (94b) shows the nasal segment receiving [dorsal] as a default place since /h/ presumably does not have any place features. The suffix /i/ should have scope over the reciprocal affix since /i/ is not treated as the end segment for the back loop. This indicates that the suffix was not spelled-out at the time the readjustment rule that adds the back link applied.

    (94c-e) present linearizations of (94b) and the arrows that show precedence relations have been suppressed for reasons of space. (94c) is the correct linearization of (94b) and this indicates that the [# → h] link is followed first. This is a non-local decision that supports the idea that linearization is an optimization process. If linearization only used local information in making decisions about which links to follow, we would expect (94d) to be the occurring linearized form since the [# → m] link is "newer" than the [# → h] link. Only by considering the whole precedence graph and realizing that initially choosing the [# → h] link results in an output that utilizes the [t → m] back link in a shorter distance of precedence relations will (94c) be produced. Two additional benefits of this optimization choice are that (94c) is a smaller precedence graph than (94d) and that an additional link (namely the [# → h] link) is used in (94c) but not (94d). All of these characteristics make (94c) a more economical linearization than (94d). Finally, (94e) shows that the requirement to utilize morphological links prevents the newest precedence information added by the suffix /i/ from overriding other older morphological information. This point also rules out other possible linearization paths through (94b) such as *hormat*, *hormati*, and *məŋhormat*.

Returning to interposed forms that show nasal substitution effects, the presence of the jump link added by the rule in (92) explains the lack of an appearance of overapplication. Consider the possible linearizations of the precedence graph in (93b) presented below in (95).

(95) a.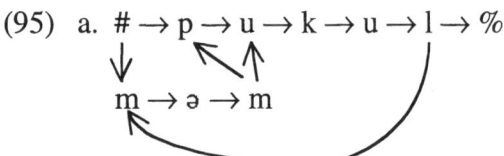

    b. pukul-məm-ukul
    c. *məm-ukul-məm-pukul
    d. *məm-pukul-məm-ukul
    e. *məm-ukul-məm-ukul
    f. *pukul-məm-pukul

(95a) repeats the precedence structure in (93b) that is to be linearized. (95b) is the occurring linearized form. The [# → p] link is followed first so the [l → m] back link can be used a soon as possible just as in the linearization of *hormat-məŋ-hormati* in (94). The addition of the jump link from [m → u] overrides the [m → p] link because the [m → u] link is more recently added information. Utilizing one link from a morpheme to another morpheme is apparently sufficient to satisfy the principle of utilizing morphological links since the unused [m → p] does not cause another repetition of seg-mental material as the non-occurring form *pukul-məm-ukul-məm-pukul* shows. (95c) is a less economical linearization of (95a) than (95b) because a longer precedence distance is traveled before the [l → m] link is used. (95c) is also a larger form and does not use the [# → p] link as (95b) does. (95d,e) are less economical than (95b) for the same reasons that (95c) is less economical than (95b). Fi-nally, (95f) is less economical than (95b) because (95f) uses the older [m → p] link instead of the more recently added [m → u] link.

Both the preposed forms in (82b) and the interposed forms in (82c) have now been accounted for. In this analysis there appears to be a certain amount of conspiracy since two different rules have been utilized to characterize the nasal substitution process. There is no conspiracy between the coalescence and jump link rules if we carefully consider what their relationship is. Consider both rules again, presented in (96).

(96) a. *coalescence*   b. *jump link*

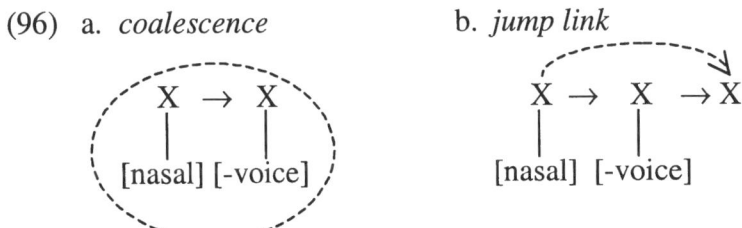

The Elsewhere Condition (Kiparsky 1973, Halle and Idsardi 1997) will govern the interaction between the two rules in (96) since the environment specified in (96a) is properly included in the environment specified in (96b). The Elsewhere Condition will require that (96a) and (96b) apply disjunctively. Specifically, since (96b) is the more specific rule it will have the first chance to apply and only if (96b) does not apply will (96a) receive a chance to apply. This re-lationship between (96a) and (96b) immediately accounts for the interposed reduplication patterns in Indonesian. Since the jump link rule of (96b) applies in these forms, no application of the coales-cence rule in (96b) will occur since it is blocked by the Elsewhere Condition.

In order to complete the analysis of the preposed reduplication pattern in Indonesian we must explain why the jump link rule in (96b) does not apply to these forms. Since (96b) does not apply, the coalescence rule in (96a) applies producing overapplication of nasal substitution seen in the preposed forms. Why the coalescence rule does not apply in the preposed forms can be explained by the Uniformity Parameter if the precedence structures at the junction between the prefix /məN/ and the stem are considered. Consider the precedence and morpho-syntactic structures for a preposed and interposed form in (97).

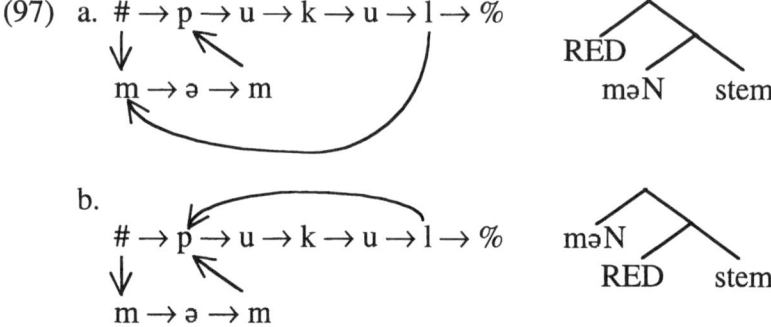

(97) a. # → p → u → k → u → l → %

m → ə → m

RED   məN   stem

b.

→ p → u → k → u → l → %

m → ə → m

məN   RED   stem

(97a) shows the precedence structure for what will result in an interposed reduplication pattern. The concatenation of the /məN/ morpheme produces a uniform precedence structure that satisfies the Derived Environment Condition. The Derived Environment Condition is satisfied because segmental material from one morpheme is preceding segmental material from another different morpheme and this relationship is uniform. (97b) has a similar relationship between /məN/ and the stem but there is a crucial difference. Since the back link added by the readjustment rule is anchored to /p/, this disrupts the uniformity of the satisfaction of the Derived Environment Condition. Since this back link connects /l/ to /p/, this link does not satisfy the Derived Environment Condition because it connects segmental material from a single morpheme. Since the Derived Environment Condition is not satisfied by all precedence links into /p/ in (97b), the application of jump link rule in (96b) is blocked thus giving the coalescence rule in (96a) a chance to apply.

In other words, by specifying the Uniformity Parameter to *on* for the jump link rule in (96b) the link added by the total reduplication readjustment rule in Indonesian will block the application of (96b) because the link added by this rule does not satisfy the Derived Environment Condition also active on this rule.

The last note on this explanation of the interaction between the jump link and coalescence rule in Indonesian is discuss why the [# → ...] link does not appear to affect the calculation on whether the Derived Environment Condition is satisfied on a rule or not. A tentative explanation is to derive the inertness of # with respect to the Derived Environment Condition from the idea of segmenthood. Since it has been repeatedly shown that the Derived Environment Condition evaluates whether segments from different morphemes have been linked via a precedence relation, the fact that # is not a segment will remove it from consideration by the Derived Environment Condition. This point completes the analysis of total reduplication in Indonesian.

The analysis presented here for the Indonesian interposed and preposed reduplication patterns is a complex one that utilizes many aspects of other analyses presented in earlier sections of this book. The complexity of the interaction of simple processes in the analysis presented here may partially obscure its merit. The analysis presented in McCarthy and Prince (1995:334-335) is very simple and therefore at the surface, it appears to be superior. This is not the case. McCarthy and Prince derive the difference in behavior of preposed and interposed reduplication on the stipulation that /məN/ is added as a suffix to the base in the interposed forms and prefixed to the base in the preposed forms.

McCarthy and Prince's stipulation that /məN/ is sometimes a suffix is not supported by any facts. There is no evidence to support this claim other than their analysis which requires this stipulation. Because of this, the analysis presented here is superior because it falls out from general principles of the model of reduplication used. No unmotivated stipulations are required in the analysis developed here other than the phonological representations that are stored in the lexicon for each morpheme. The utilization of both a coalescence rule and a jump link rule is independently motivated by other languages that have these rules. The Chumash example in chapter 2 shows the presence of the coalescence rule to cause deletion and the analysis of Tohono O'odham presented in the next section will present a case of the jump link rule accounting for the behavior of a deletion process. The interaction and functional unity of these two rules is captured by the Elsewhere Condition so it is not surprising to find a language that has both of these rules applying disjunctively to create a complex surface pattern of effects. Each part of the analysis presented here and the interaction of these parts is accounted for by language universal principles such as morphological scope, the Derived Environment Condition, and the Elsewhere Condition. The complex pattern of the preposed and interposed reduplication pattern in Indonesian results from the interaction of individually simple processes that interact to create the complicated surface effects.

3.4.2 CV reduplication

Tohono O'odham uses reduplication to mark plural and plural agreement on verbs, nouns, adjectives, and adverbs. The main pattern of plural reduplication is CV as seen in (98) which presents data drawn from Saxton, Saxton and Enos (1989) and Zepeda (1983).

(98)	ʔum	ʔu-ʔum	'a thigh'
	ʔat	ʔa-ʔat	'the anus'
	hon	ho-hon	'the body'
	bawi	ba-bawi	'the tepary bean (dist.)'
	gimai	gi-gimai	'a braggart'
	ɲɨo	ɲɨ-ɲɨo	'to speak (perfective)'
	pualt	pu-pualt	'a door'
	ʝioʃ	ʝi-ʝioʃ	'a god'
	podoni	popodoni	'to thump'

Given this pattern of reduplication it would be expected that the back link would connect the first vowel to the first segment of the word but this is not quite correct. The forms in (99) show that words which begin with a consonant cluster behave in a slightly different manner.

(99) tlaamba   t-la-lamba 'a tramp'
     plaanja   p-la-lanja 'iron'
     klaawo   k-la-lwo   'a nail'
     ploomo   p-lo-lmo   'lead (the metal)'
     tloogii   t-lo-logii 'a truck'

The difference between the forms in (98) and (99) is that reduplication acts as an infix in (99) instead of acting like a prefix as in forms in (98). This behavior can be captured by specifying the precedence variables for this affix as in (100).

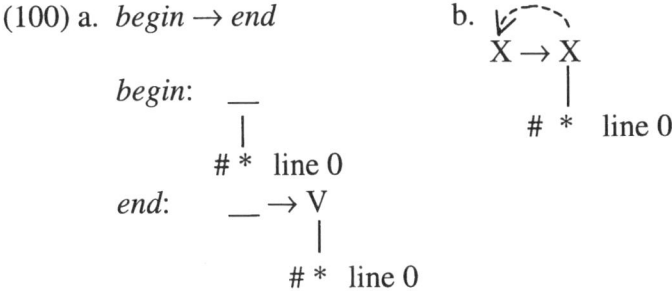

(100) states that the first vowel precedes the segment which precedes the first vowel. This will produce a loop in a formative that will result in CV reduplication that will infix when there is a consonant cluster in word initial position.

The data in (101) show an additional aspect of CV reduplication in Tohono O'odham. These forms have a "weakening" of the vowel in the base of reduplicated forms. The behavior of this process in stems with short vowels, (101a), and diphthongs, (101b) is presented below.

(101) a. ʔaʔag   ʔa-ʔʔag   'the brain (dist.)'
         babað   ba-bbað   'a frog (dist.)'
         čipkan   či-čpkan   'working'

gaso	ga-gso	'a fox'
maskal	ma-mskal	'a bandana'

b.
doakag	do-dakag	'a life'
koa	ko-ka	'the forehead'
čɨadagi	čɨ-čadagi	'the Gila monster'
čɨoǰ	čɨ-čoǰ	'boy, man'
ɲɨok	ɲɨ-ɲok	'talking- imperfective'

(101a) shows forms with short vowels in their base and the reduplication patterns shows deletion of these vowels. (101b) shows forms with diphthongs and the weakening process appears to split the diphthong between the reduplicant and the base. Both of these behaviors can be accounted for by a jump link rule of the form in (102) which states that a link will be added from the segment preceding the first vowel to the segment that follows the first vowel. The effect of this link is to jump over the first vowel during linearization which results in the surface deletion of it. (102) is a readjustment rule that individual lexical forms are marked as to undergo it or not. There does not appear to be any way of predicting which forms undergo this rule.

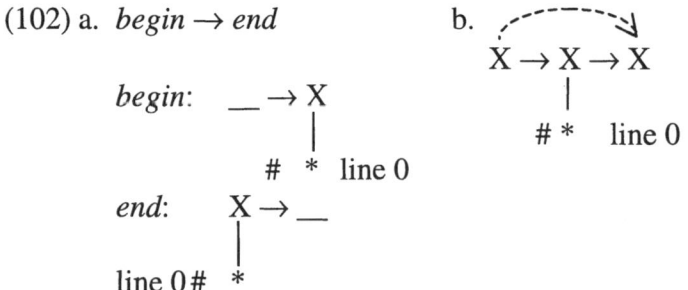

(103) shows the construction of the phonological representation of a short vowelled form that has the additional jump link.

(103) a. # → b → a → b → a → ð̆ → %

b. # → b → a → b → a → ð̆ → %

c. $\# \rightarrow b \rightarrow a \rightarrow b \rightarrow a \rightarrow \eth \rightarrow \%$

d. $\# \rightarrow b \rightarrow a \rightarrow b \rightarrow b \rightarrow a \rightarrow \eth \rightarrow \%$

The ordering of the application of the reduplication readjustment from (100) and the jump link in (102) is irrelevant because both rules make reference to the word initial vowel via the metrical grid. There will be no ambiguity of reference caused by the application of both of these rules since the calculation of the first vowel on the metrical grid is not affected by either rule.

The linearization of (103c) is relatively simple in that following the jump link must be delayed until the back link is followed. This choice is driven by the principle to spell out as many morphological links as possible.

The jump link approach to the deletion of some vowels in reduplicated forms has the added benefit that it illuminates a distinction between two possible representations of long vowels. (104) shows that long vowels behave in two different ways when the jump link is added.

(104) a.

ʔaagli	ʔa-ʔagli	'an acre'
bool	bo-bol	'a ball'
čaagii	ča-čagii	'a bank'
hɨɨgig	hɨ-hɨgig	'happiness'
hii	hihi	'walking'

b.

baabas	ba-bbas	'a potato'
čɨɨgig	čɨ-čgig	'name'
giiko	gi-gko	'a crown'
looba	lo-lba	'dry goods'

The forms in (104a) show a long vowel in the base being shortened while the forms in (104b) present cases where the long vowel is deleted entirely in the base.

The different behavior of the long vowels in (104) can be derived from how a long vowel is represented. Long vowels can be represented either by a self-loop, (105a), or by the traditional single melody linked to two timing slots approach, (105b).

(105) a. 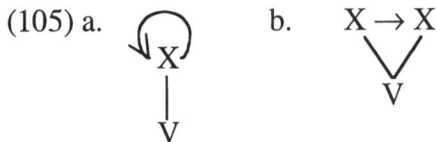 b.

Given the possibility of two different types of long vowels, the different behavior of long vowels seen in (104) is directly captured by treating the long vowels in (104a) as traditional geminate structures and the long vowels in (104b) as self-looped vowels.

A derivation of a vowel with a traditional geminate representation is presented in (106). Due to this representation, this type of long vowel behaves in the same way as the diphthong vowels in (101b).

(106)   a. # → b → o → o → l → %

        b. # → b → o → o → l → %

        c. # → b → o → o → l → %

Since the long vowel has two distinct timing units the jump link will identify the second part of the long vowel as following the first vowel. This results in a precedence structure similar to the one in (102c) which derived the behavior of stems with short vowels. Linearization of (105c) is identical to the linearization of (102c).

A representation with a long vowel represented by a self-loop behaves differently. Because the long vowel loops back onto itself, the jump link skips entirely over this vowel. Consider the representations in (107).

(107) a.

        # → b → a → b → a → s → %

b.

$$\# \rightarrow b \xrightarrow{} a \xrightarrow{} b \rightarrow a \rightarrow s \rightarrow \%$$

c.

$$\# \rightarrow b \xrightarrow{} a \xrightarrow{} b \rightarrow a \rightarrow s \rightarrow \%$$

d. $\# \rightarrow b \rightarrow a \rightarrow b \rightarrow b \rightarrow a \rightarrow s \rightarrow \%$

The jump link added by the readjustment rule in (102) does not
vacuously link /b/ to /a/ in (107b) because the /a/ is identified as the
first vowel. (102) specifies a beginning and end of an added precedence link. The beginning of the added precedence link is the timing unit that precedes the timing unit associated with the first
vowel. The end of the added precedence link is the timing unit that
follows the timing unit of the first vowel. Since the long vowel in
(107) is represented by a single timing unit that is repeated via the
self-loop, this timing unit associated with the first vowel can not
satisfy the environment for the end of the added link. This is another point that distinguishes between the representations of long
vowels in (105). Given this point about how the representation of
long vowels interacts with (102), the remainder of the concatenation of affixes in (107) is the same as in (106).

The linearization of (107c) presents a case where a lexical link is
not followed because of morphological pressure. As in the linearization of interposed forms in Indonesian, global information is
utilized by the linearization process. This can be seen in two different decision points in the linearization. The first decision point is to
delay following the jump link added by (102) until the back link
added by (100) is followed. If the jump link is followed immediately then the back link will not be followed at all and this violates
the goal of using all added links. The second decision point is when
the first vowel is reached. Should the vowel go back to itself following the lexical link or back to the /b/ following the link added by
(102)? The pressure to use morphologically added material first
causes the back link to be followed just as in the Indonesian interposed forms. Once again at the beginning of the precedence graph,

since the back link has already been used, the jump link receives priority and is followed leading to a straightforward linearization of the remainder of the graph. The result of this process is the occurring surface form in (107d).

The linearization effect that long vowels get shortened in precedence structures as in (107c) draws attention to another subpattern of reduplication in Tohono O'odham. There is a group of forms that show CV reduplication with the vowel in the reduplicant being long. Consider the data in (108).

(108) a. toon   too-ton   'knee'
         kaam   kaa-kam   'a cheek...'
         kii   kii-ki   'a house'
         taad   taa-tad   'foot'
         baab   baa-bab   'grandfather'

     b. kuuðagi   kuu-kðagi   'a firebrand'
         ʃaakim   ʃaa-ʃkim   'a halter for a horse'
         ðaak   ðaa-ðk   'nose'
         maawua   maa-mwua   'put a hand...'
         naak   naa-nk   'an ear'

     c. ʔulin   ʔuu-ʔulin   'hold'
         ban   baa-ban   'coyote'
         čiɲ   čii-čiɲ   'mouth'
         ɟɨg   ɟɨɨ-ɟɨg   'outside'
         kun   kuu-kun   'husband'

The forms in (108a,b) are analogous to the forms in (104a,b) with respect to the representation of long vowels. The difference between these sets of forms is that in (108a,b) there is a long vowel in the reduplicant. This should not be the case if the linearization of (107c) is correct.

The linearization of (107c) indicates that some lexical precedence links are bypassed in favor of using added links. The skipping of some lexical links explains why there is shortening or deletion of the vowel in the base of forms in (104) when other added links are present. Consequently, the forms in (108a,b) appear to be-have differently because the lexical links that are skipped in the forms in (104) are followed in the linearizations of the forms in (108a,b). This linearization paradox can be resolved if the forms in (108c) which show lengthening of a short vowel in the reduplicant are considered.

The stems with short vowels that show vowel lengthening in (108c) can be accounted for by adding a readjustment rule that adds a self-loop onto the first vowel. This rule can be formalized as in (109).

(109) a. *begin → end*   b.

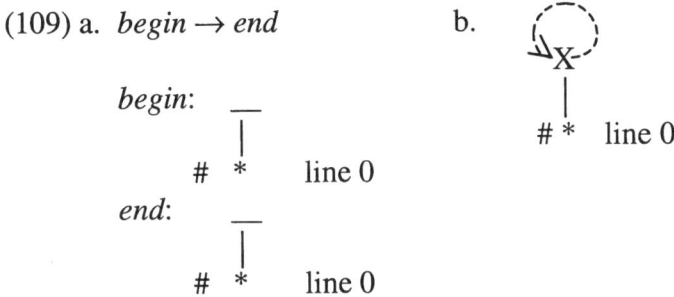

     begin: —
                  |
            #   *   line 0

     end: —
                  |
            #   *   line 0

The morphological spell-out of a form with a short vowel and the added self-loop creates representations as in (110).

(110) a. # → b → a → n → %

b. # → b ⇝ a ⇝ n → %

c. # → b ⇝ a ⇝ n → %

Linearization of (110c) shows that the added self-loop is followed before the back link is because it results in a linearization that dis-charges the added links quicker than other possible linearizations. If the back link were followed first then a form with a long vowel in the stem would result. This is a less economical linearization than

the occurring surface form because it takes travelling five precedence links to discharge all added links as opposed to the occurring
linearization that only requires four precedence links to discharge
these links. This comparison is shown in (111) with added links in
outline.

(111) a. # → b → a ⇒ a ⇒ b → ...

b. # → b → a ⇒ b → a ⇒ a →...

Both of the added links in (110c) are used by the fourth step in
(111a). (111b) shows that following the added links in the opposite
ordering requires five steps to utilize both of them.

The self-loop readjustment rule also directly accounts for the
long vowel forms in (108a,b). Forms with long vowels represented
as geminates, as in (108a), behave in the same way as (110c). Long
vowels represented as self-loops undergo the derivation in (112).

(112) a.

→ n → a → k → %

b.

→ n → a → k → %

c.

→ n → a → k → %

d.

→ n → a → k → %

The fact that one of the self-loops in (112d) is lexical and one is
morphological explains the surface form where a long vowel ap-

pears in the reduplicant and no vowel appears in the base. The morphological loop causes the linearization to proceed as it did in (110c). As in the earlier long vowel self-loop forms, the lexical loop is skipped to create a shorter output form.

To complete the discussion of the long vowel CV reduplication pattern in Tohono O'odham, we should note that there are short vowel bases that undergo both readjustment rules, (102) and (109), to produce a surface pattern of lengthening in the reduplicant and deletion in the base. A few of these forms are presented in (113). /w/ turns to /p/ when it is word internal in some forms.

(113)	čukud	čuu-čkud	'an owl'
	tatal	taa-ttal	'an uncle...'
	wuhio	wuu-phio	'face to face (adv.)'
	wulim	wuu-plim	'a bale'
	ðahiwuia	ðaa-ðhiwuia	'a kangaroo'

The final alternative pattern of reduplication in Tohono O'odham that will be discussed is one where a /VʔV/ sequence is added to the stem. This modification behaves in a similar manner to the long vowel self-loop rule in (109). Consider the data in (114) which shows the interaction of the /VʔV/ reduplication pattern and types of bases.

(114) a.	waik	waʔa-waik	'(a) three'
	wɨčo	wɨʔɨ-wɨčo	'under'
	pad	paʔa-pad	'badly'
	topiðk	toʔo-topiðk	'(be) askew'
b.	napad	naʔa npad	'sprawled'
	ʃapɨj	ʃaʔa-ʃpɨj	'narrow'
	sikol	siʔi-skol	'(be) circular'
	waðaðk	waʔa-pðaðk	'be shiny'
	komad	koʔo-kmad	'in a spread...'
c.	toonk	toʔo-tonk	'a dike...'
	gook	goʔo-gok	'(a) two'

kuugam	kuʔu-kugam	'backward'
taagio	taʔa-tagio	'in front of...'
ʃaagiծ	ʃaʔa-ʃagiծ	'between (dist.)'

(114a) shows the /VʔV/ pattern with forms that have a short vowel or diphthong without a jump link. (114b) show the /VʔV/ pattern with short vowel bases with a jump link. (114c) presents one type of long vowel base with the /VʔV/ readjustment. The /VʔV/ reduplication pattern can be accounted for by the readjustment rule in (115) in addition to the normal CV reduplication readjustment in Tohono O'odham.

(115) a. *begin* → ʔ → *end*   b.

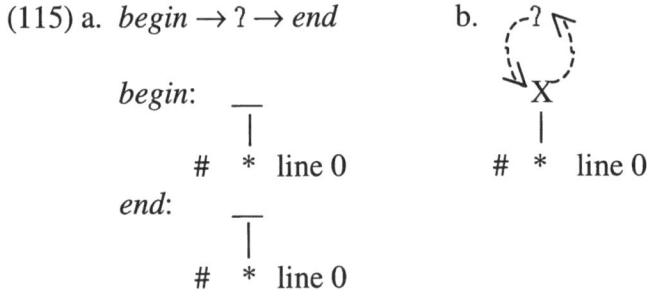

The interaction of (115) with the jump link readjustment rule, long vowels of both types, short vowels, and CV reduplication in Tohono O'odham is the same as the self-loop long vowel readjustment rule in (109).

   This completes an analysis of the patterns of CV reduplication in Tohono O'odham based on the proposals in this book. Now that an analysis has been presented we can compare it with other analyses. The first competing analysis is one based in Optimality Theory offered by Fitzgerald (to appear). Fitzgerald proposes to account for the splitting of diphthongs in (101b) in some reduplicated forms by positing the constraint in (116).

(116) *HL[+RD]: For a sequence $V_x V_{x+1}$ where one of the two vowels is [+round], the height of V_x must not be greater than the height of V_{x+1}.

The constraint in (116) is meant to provide a generalization as to when a vowel is deleted in the base of reduplicated forms with diphthongs. To illustrate the merit of this constraint and how it is ranked with respect to other constraints in Tohono O'odham, Fitzgerald presents the tableau in (117).

(117)

/RED-$\check{c}_1u_2a_3m_4a_5$/	RED$_{CV}$	MAX$_{IO}$	*HL[+RD]	CONT$_{IR}$	CONT$_{IB}$
a. $\check{c}_1u_2$-$\check{c}_1u_2a_3m_4a_5$			*!		
☞ b. $\check{c}_1u_2$-$\check{c}_1a_3m_4a_5$					*
c. $\check{c}_1u_2$-$\check{c}_1a_3m_4$		*!			*

The constraint RED$_{CV}$ is a cover constraint for the constraints that interact to produce a CV reduplicant, MAX$_{IO}$ is the correspondence theory (McCarthy and Prince 1995) constraint that requires all segments in the input to have a correspondent in the output, and CONT$_{IR}$ (reduplicant) and CONT$_{IB}$ (base) are constraints that penalize outputs that diverge from the precedence structure of the input with respect to contiguity.

Candidate (117a) violates the *HL[+RD] constraint proposed by Fitzgerald (to appear) since a diphthong that satisfies the description of *HL[+RD] occurs in the output. Candidate (117b) does not violate *HL[+RD] because a vowel has been deleted from the base. This deletion does not violate MAX$_{IO}$ because MAX$_{IO}$ considers the entire output form in evaluating whether a segment has a correspondent or not (Raimy and Idsardi 1997, Struijke 1998). Candidate (117c) does violate MAX$_{IO}$ since there is no correspondent in the output for the input segment /a_5/. Given the particular ranking in (117), candidate (117b) is the most harmonic.

The analysis proposed by Fitzgerald is clearly inferior to the present one because only a subset of the data covered here is accounted for by Fitzgerald (to appear). The *HL[+RD] constraint in (116) will not account for the different behavior of long vowels in bases or the other patterns of reduplication that result from additional readjustment rules. Consider bases that contain long vowels in the tableaux in (118-119).

(118)

/RED-$b_1o_2o_3l_4$/	RED$_{CV}$	MAX$_{IO}$	*HL[+RD]	CONT$_{IR}$	CONT$_{IB}$
☛ a. b_1o_2-$b_1o_2o_3l_4$					
☞ b. b_1o_2-$b_1o_2l_4$					*!
☞ c. b_1o_2-$b_1o_3l_4$					*!

(119)

/RED-$l_1o_2o_3b_4a_5$/	RED$_{CV}$	MAX$_{IO}$	*HL[+RD]	CONT$_{IR}$	CONT$_{IB}$
☛ a. l_1o_2-$l_1o_2o_3b_4a_5$					
b. l_1o_2-$l_1o_3b_4a_5$					*!
☞ c. l_1o_2-$l_1b_4a_5$		*!			*

The tableaux in (118-119) show that there is no motivation for the modifications to the base in forms with long vowels in the base. The black hand (☛) indicates the most harmonic candidates in (118-119) although they are not the occurring surface forms. The occurring surface forms are indicated by the white hands (☞). It is not obvious how to expand Fitzgerald's proposed analysis to include the patterns of bases with long vowels, short vowel bases that show deletion of the vowel in the base, and the /VʔV/ reduplication patterns.

On a more specific note, the proposed *HL[+RD] constraint is problematic for three reasons. The first problem is that this constraint is not a realistic one. It must be decomposed into the conjunction of simpler constraints but it is not clear exactly which constraints should be conjoined to create the effect of *HL[+RD].

The second problem is that *HL[+RD] is too in narrow scope. This constraint misses the connection between the deletion of vowels in the bases in all forms (long vowels, short vowels, diphthongs, etc.) that is established in the present analysis. Deletion of vowels in the base results from the application of a readjustment rule that adds a jump link. This single rule accounts for the deletions of vowels in all types of forms. It is unclear as to how Fitzgerald could modify her analysis to make the "jump link generalization" without totally recapitulating the present analysis within Optimality Theory.

Finally, *HL[+RD] is also too broad in scope. This constraint claims that all sequences of these particular diphthongs should behave as the tableau in (117) indicates. This is a false prediction. Consider the tableaux in (120-121).

(120)

/RED-$\text{ɲ}_1\text{i}_2\text{o}_3$/	RED_{CV}	MAX_{IO}	*HL[+RD]	CONT_{IR}	CONT_{IB}
☞ a. $\text{ɲ}_1\text{i}_2\text{-ɲ}_1\text{i}_2\text{o}_3$			*!		
☛ b. $\text{ɲ}_1\text{i}_2\text{-ɲ}_1\text{o}_3$					*

(121)

/$\text{s}_1\text{i}_2\text{b}_3\text{i}_4\text{o}_5$/	RED_{CV}	MAX_{IO}	*HL[+RD]	CONT_{IR}	CONT_{IB}
☞ a. $\text{s}_1\text{i}_2\text{b}_3\text{i}_4\text{o}_5$			*!		
b. $\text{s}_1\text{i}_2\text{b}_3\text{i}_4$		*!			
c. $\text{s}_1\text{i}_2\text{b}_3\text{o}_5$		*!			*
☛ d. $\text{s}_1\text{i}_2\text{b}_3\text{o}_5\text{i}_4$					*

The form in tableau (120) shows that *HL[+RD] is a spurious phonological generalization. Whether a form that contains a diphthong in the base deletes a vowel in the base is an arbitrary lexical fact. This conclusion is supported by the near minimal pair *ɲio* > *ɲi-ɲio* and *ɲiok* > *ɲi-ɲok* and their reduplicants. Both forms come from the same root (meaning 'to speak') with the difference being that *ɲiok* is imperfective and *ɲio* is perfective (Zepeda 1983:59). This is a morphological difference that is a natural source for the application of a readjustment rule or not which lends support to the analysis presented here. A phonological analysis such as the one presented by Fitzgerald (to appear) is unable to explain the difference in near minimal pairs such as these.

Tableau (121) points out the fact that if *HL[+RD] is ranked above CONT_{IB} (which evaluates contiguity of the input vs. the contiguity of the entire output) there should be no surface violations of *HL[+RD] at all in Tohono O'odham. (121) is a tableau presented by Fitzgerald (to appear:fn 8) with an added candidate. Candidate (121d) that metathesizes the diphthong to avoid violation of *HL[+RD] is the most harmonic candidate given the present constraint ranking. Unfortunately, candidate (121a) is the occurring form so it can be seen that the analysis presented by Fitzgerald (to appear) has difficulties in accounting for the entire set of data.

A prosodic analysis of vowel syncope (jumping behavior in the present analysis) is proposed by Hill and Zepeda (1992). This prosodic account is similar to Fitzgerald (to appear) in that it claims that the different patterns of reduplication in Tohono O'odham is phonologically predictable. Any phonological analysis of reduplication cannot distinguish between near minimal pairs where jumping occurs in one form but not the other (i.e. *ɲiok* > *ɲiɲok*, *ɲio* > *ɲiɲio* 'to speak' imperfective vs. perfective). The prosodic constraint proposed by Hill and Zepeda to account for long vowel reduplication is inadequate because of prosodic minimal pairs where a long vowel reduplicant appears in one but not the other (i.e. *ʔum* > *ʔuʔum* 'a thigh' vs. *ban* > *baaban* 'coyote', *bawi* > *babawi* 'the tepary bean' vs. *čini* > *čiičini* 'a mouth', *ʔikus* > *ʔiʔikus* 'cloth' vs. *ʔulin* > *ʔuuʔulin* 'to hold (something) out'). Again, this type of minimal pair supports the claim of the analysis presented here that the different patterns of reduplication in Tohono O'odham result from lexically controlled readjustment rules.

In contrast to these two other analyses the present analysis provides the following benefits. Broad observational adequacy of Tohono O'odham CV reduplication is achieved because all of the reduplicated forms in Saxton, Saxton and Enos (1989) and Zepeda (1983) are accounted for. The representational difference in long vowels developed here reduces apparent exceptions because no diacritic is used. Only language universal representational differences are utilized. Universal grammar provides both the self-loop representation and the traditional geminate representation as possibilities in representing a long segment.[14] One aspect of learning a language that has long segments is determining which of these two possible representations of "long" should be used. Tohono O'odham presents the interesting case where both types of long representations are utilized and whether a long vowel is a self-looped vowel or a geminate vowel can be determined by how the vowel in question interacts with the jump link rule.

The present analysis also provides a single generalization for plural reduplication in Tohono O'odham. The CV link that is added by the readjustment rule in (100) applies to all forms that have the plural morpheme. Subsidiary patterns of reduplication that appear

to deviate from CV reduplication are derived from lexically specified readjustment rules. The specific CV link that is added also appears in Bella Coola (Newman 1971, Nater 1984, 1991, Raimy and
Idsardi 1997) where internal CV reduplication also occurs as the
result of consonant clusters at the beginning of a word (i.e. *skma* >
s-km-kma 'moose'/'moose diminuative', *tup* > *tu-tup* 'spot-
ted'/'trout'). Utilizing readjustment rules to account for lexically
determined subpatterns have independent motivation going back to
The sound pattern of English (Chomsky and Halle 1968). The
analysis of Tohono O'odham presented here provides strong evidence that no cophonology or multiple reduplication morphemes
are needed to account for the reduplication patterns in Tohono
O'odham. The surface complexity of these reduplication patterns is
derived from the interaction of simple rules.

3.4.3 CVC Reduplication[15]

Another common pattern of reduplication follows a CVC template.
The most interesting feature of this type of reduplication is that it
usually ignores syllabic constituency in that sometimes a coda is
copied in order to satisfy the CVC template while in other cases the
onset of a following syllable is copied. An example of this type of
reduplication from Agta (taken from Marantz 1982:449) shows how
this template type can be easily accounted for within the present
framework. The basic pattern of CVC reduplication in Agta is presented in (122).

(122) takki   'leg'   tak-takki   'legs'
      uffu   'thigh'   uf-uffu   'thighs'
      bari   'body'   bar-bari   'my whole body'
      na-wakay   'lost'   na-wak-wakay   'many things lost'

The data in (122) indicate that Agta reduplicates the first CVC sequence of a root regardless of the syllabic association of the second
C. Note that whether the root is consonant or vowel initial does not
affect the pattern. More neutrally, this pattern can be described as

"copy up to the first consonant after a vowel". This pattern of reduplication can be produced by the precedence link in (123).

(123) a. *begin → end*

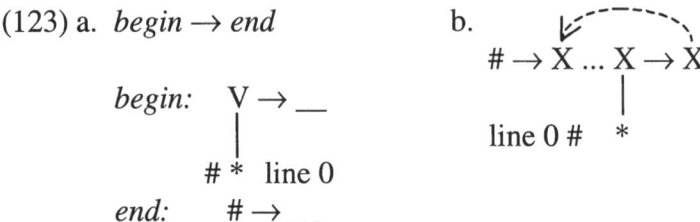

    begin: V → __

               |

            # * line 0

    end: # → __

(123) indicates that the added precedence link will link whatever follows the first vowel and whatever the first segment is. Note that in vowel initial forms, the first vowel and first segment are the same entity (i.e. *uffi > uf-uffi*).

A very similar pattern of CVC reduplication is found in Ilokano heavy reduplication but there is a slight twist to the data. (124) shows that for some forms the behavior of Ilokano heavy reduplication is identical to Agta but for other forms a slightly different pattern emerges. The data in (124) is taken from Hayes and Abad (1989:357-359) and heavy reduplication is used to mark both plural on nouns and progressive aspect on verbs. This polysemy supports the view that reduplication results from a readjustment rule. Following this point, plural is a zero morph in Ilokano that triggers the reduplication readjustment rule. The primary exponence of progressive aspect is the prefix /ʔag/ which also triggers the reduplication readjustment.

(124) a. kaldíŋ   'goat'   kal-kaldíŋ   'goats'

         púsa   'cat'   pus-púsa   'cats'

         ǰyánitor 'janitor'   ǰyan-ǰyanitor   'janitors'

         sáŋit   'to cry'   ʔag-saŋ-sáŋit   'is crying'

         trabáho 'to work'   ʔag-trab-trabáho 'is working'

     b. dáʔit   'to sew'   ʔag-daa-dáʔit   'is sewing'

        róʔot   'leaves'   roo-róʔot   'leaves (pl.)'

        paʔíd   'fan'   paa-paʔíd   'fans'

c. trák	'truck'	traa-trák	'trucks'
bás	'bus'	baa-bás	'buses'
nyáw	'to meow'	?ag-nyaa-nyáw	'is meowing'

The main difference between Agta and Ilokano is seen in (124b,c). (124b) shows that in forms where the first vowel is followed by a glottal stop, only the onset and first vowel are copied accompanied by the lengthening of the copied vowel. (124c) shows that mono-syllabic forms behave like the forms in (124b). Heavy reduplication in Ilokano can be characterized by (125) and (126).

(125)   *begin* → X → *end*

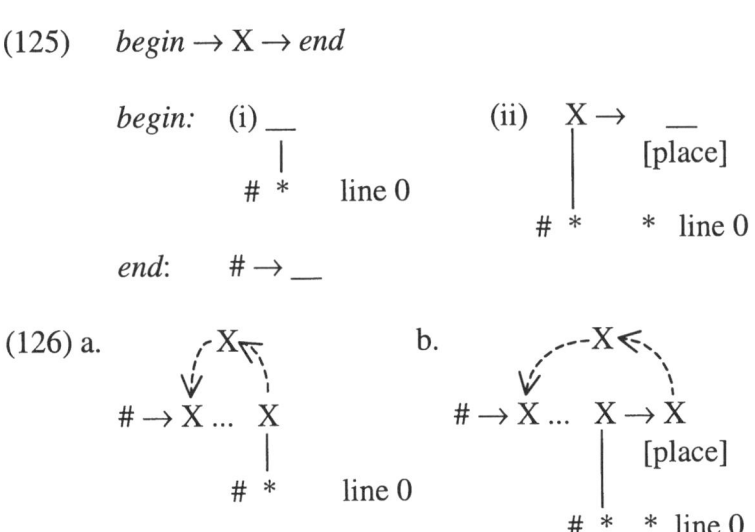

The differences between (123) and (125/126) are as follows. To begin, the beginning precedence variable in (125/126) has a two clause environment that specifies where this link should concatenate. In (125) the (i) clause *begin* environment specifies the first vowel and the (ii) clause *begin* environment specifies a consonant with place features that follows the first vowel which is followed by a vowel. These two environments are governed by the Elsewhere Condition (Kiparsky 1973) so that the (i) clause will be blocked by the more specific (ii) clause. Additionally, there is an empty X-slot that is part of the phonological representation of heavy reduplication in Ilokano. This X-slot accounts for the lengthening behavior of some forms. Lengthening is not surface apparent in all forms because of syllabification restrictions that sometimes eliminate the morphological lengthening.

The same information about what link is added according to the heavy reduplication readjustment rule is in (126a,b). (126a) presents the general case and (126b) presents the more specific case. The relationship between these two rules is a bit clearer since the parts of the environments that are shared between them are readily apparent.

To see how the rule in (125/126) works, consider the derivations in (127) and (128) that show how the Ilokano facts are captured by these rules. Note that unlike previous examples in this book, the melody/timing slot distinction is crucial so these will be represented autosegmentally in (127-128).

(127) a. $\# \to X \to X \to X \to X \to X \to \%$
$\qquad$ r $\quad$ o $\quad$? $\quad$ o $\quad$ t

b. $\# \to X \to X \to X \to X \to X \to \%$
$\qquad$ r $\quad$ o $\quad$? $\quad$ o $\quad$ t

c. $\# \to X \to X \to X \to X \to X \to \%$
$\qquad$ r $\quad$ o $\quad$? $\quad$ o $\quad$ t

d. $\# \to r \to o \to o \to r \to o \to ? \to o \to t \to \%$

(127a) shows the base that (125/126) searches on to determine where the beginning precedence variable should concatenate. Since the first vowel in (127a) is not followed by a consonant with a place feature, the beginning precedence variable concatenates to the first vowel producing (127b). (127c) shows the features from the first vowel spreading into the empty X-slot and (127d) shows the resulting linearized form that shows vowel lengthening.

(128) a. $\# \rightarrow X \rightarrow X \rightarrow X \rightarrow X \rightarrow \%$

$\qquad$ p   u   s   a

b. $\# \rightarrow X \rightarrow X \rightarrow X \rightarrow X \rightarrow \%$

$\qquad$ p   u   s   a

c. $\# \rightarrow X \rightarrow X \rightarrow X \rightarrow X \rightarrow \%$

$\qquad$ p   u   s   a

d. $\# \rightarrow p \rightarrow u \rightarrow s \rightarrow s \rightarrow p \rightarrow u \rightarrow s \rightarrow a \rightarrow \%$

e. $\# \rightarrow p \rightarrow u \rightarrow s \rightarrow p \rightarrow u \rightarrow s \rightarrow a \rightarrow \%$

(128) is slightly different in that the more specific clause of (125/126) is satisfied so the beginning precedence variable concatenates to the consonant following the first vowel. This creates the structure in (128b) and (128c) shows the spreading of the place features of /s/ into the empty X-slot. (128d) shows the linearized form and (128e) shows the degemination of /s/ presumably due to a universal tautosyllabic degemination rule.

The derivations in (127-128) show that (125/126) correctly captures the behavior of heavy reduplication in Ilokano and the slight difference between (123) and (125/126) succinctly captures both the similarity and the difference between Ilokano and Agta. The forms in (124c) that show CVV reduplication even though there is a consonant with place features following the first vowel are accounted for by the requirement in the (ii) clause in (128) that the form be disyllabic. This requirement is present in (125/126) by the additional * mark on the line 0 specification in the (ii) clause of this rule so any form with only a single vowel will not satisfy this more specific part of (125/126). This is an improvement on the analysis provided by Hayes and Abad (1989:359) since they must resort to stipulating this effect.

Evidence for the complex formulation of the more specific clause in (125/126) is found in languages that have slightly different reduplication patterns. Mokilese (Harrison 1976, Raimy to appear) has a very similar pattern of heavy syllable reduplication that only differs from Ilokano in that monosyllabic forms show CVC reduplication if they are CVC in form. This indicates that the second vowel requirement is a legitimate part of the Ilokano rule since Mokilese has the same rule without this structural requirement. Kusaiean (Lee 1975) a language related to Mokilese (Harrison 1976) provides evidence for the empty X-slot to account for the heavy syllable aspect of the Ilokano and Mokilese reduplication patterns. Kusaiean shows a similar multi-clause beginning precedence variable but no lengthening of any sort. Consider the data in (129) from Lee (1975). Note that "." mark syllable boundaries in (129).

(129) a. ku.lus   'to peel'   kul.ku.lus   'to peel bit by bit'
         ki.pat   'to fall'   kip.ki.pat   'to fall gradually'
         ti.pʌl   'to pick'   tip.ti.pʌl   'to pick again and again'
         pi.ṣik   'to flick'   piṣ.pi.ṣik   'to flick repeatedly'

     b. e.wʌ   'to lift'   ew.e.wʌ   'to lift little by little'
         i.pis   'to roll'   ip.i.pis   'to roll bit by bit'
         o.laŋ   'to open'   ol.o.laŋ   'to open again and again'

     c. kɔ.u   'grouchy'   kɔ.kɔ.u   'rather grouchy'
         mo.ul   'alive'   mo.mo.ul   'not completely dead'
         fo.ul   'smell'   fo.fo.ul   'to emit smell'

(129a) presents forms that reduplicate a CVC sequence when the base for reduplication contains a consonant following the first vowel. This is the same pattern seen in Ilokano CVC reduplication. (129b) shows vowel initial forms in Kusaiean and these forms do not show gemination of the reduplicated consonant. This contrasts with Mokilese vowel initial forms that do show gemination of the reduplicated consonant, e.g. *ir > irr-ir* 'string', *onop > onn-onop* 'prepare', *idip > idd-idip* 'draw water' due to the empty X-slot that occurs as part of the Mokilese reduplication pattern. Further evidence that Kusaiean does not have an X-slot associated with its reduplication pattern is in (129c) which shows forms that do not have a consonant following the first vowel. These forms just show CV reduplication without any lengthening of the vowel in the reduplicant and this directly contrasts with the Ilokano forms in (124b).

The slight differences in behavior among Mokilese, Ilokano, and Kusaiean calls into question the notion of an output target of heavy syllable. Each of these languages produces a heavy syllable in some reduplication patterns but these languages diverge when determining what to do if there is not a CVC sequence to copy. Both Ilokano and Mokilese contain an empty X-slot that explains why there is vowel lengthening when a CVC sequence is not reduplicated. The surface appearance of a heavy syllable goal is captured by this empty X-slot. Kusaiean does not have this X-slot and this explains why no such lengthening occurs in this language. Mokilese and Ilokano diverge from each other in that Ilokano requires bases to be disyllabic for CVC reduplication to occur where Mokilese has no such requirement. Consider the representations for each of these reduplication patterns in (130).

(130) a. Ilokano

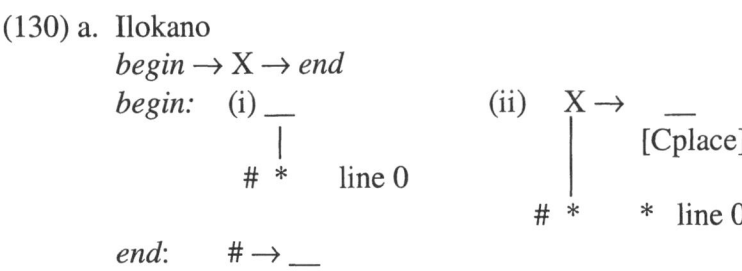

b. Mokilese
  begin → X → *end*

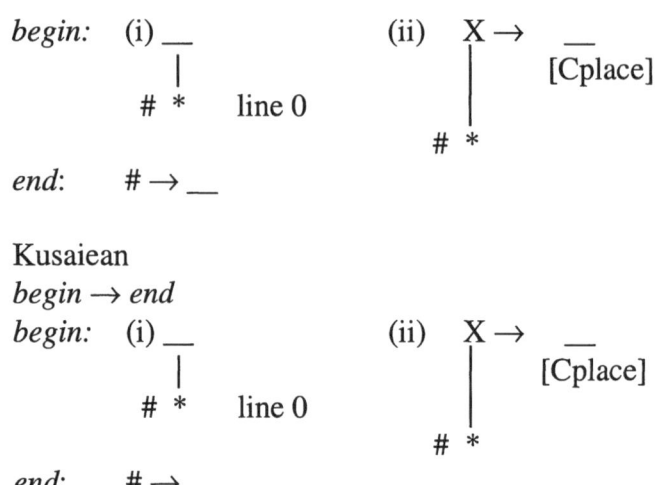

c. Kusaiean
   begin → *end*

Both the similarities and the differences in the reduplication patterns in Mokilese, Ilokano and Kusaiean are captured by the rules in
(130). The concept of heavy syllable has nothing to say about the
subtle differences encoded in the rules in (130). An analysis that
utilizes the notion of an output goal will also have to indicate what
subpatterns occur when a heavy syllable is not immediately achievable and this indicates that an output goal is not sufficient to account for heavy syllable reduplication. Since these subpatterns must
be encoded in any analysis, the fact that the present analysis encodes both the main reduplication pattern and the subpatterns without resorting to an output target indicates that output goals are not
necessary to account for heavy syllable reduplication. The combination of these two points calls into question the utility of output
goals in accounting for reduplicative templates. The analysis of Ilokano presented here indicates that heavy syllable reduplication can
be insightfully analyzed through the use of empty X-slots without
resorting to output conditions or goals.

Another argument in favor of the abandoning of surface oriented
goals in reduplication patterns is provided by Mangarrayi
(McCarthy and Prince 1986:36). This language presents a different
type of CVC reduplication in that it does not appear to be possible
to claim that the reduplicant is both contiguous and a legitimate
prosodic unit. Consider the data in (131).

(131) gabuji 'old person'   gab-ab-uji   'old persons'
      yirag   'father'   yir-ir-ag   'fathers'
      waŋgij 'child'   waŋg-aŋg-ij 'children'
      waɭima 'young person'   wa-ɭa-ɭima   'young persons'
      jimgan 'knowledgeable   jimg-img-an 'knowledgeable
              one'   ones'

The main question that this data presents is what exactly is the reduplicant in these forms. To begin with, whatever the reduplicant is, this is a case of infixing reduplication. Once this is assumed, the question is now whether the reduplicant is $VC_1(C_2)$ or $C_2V(C_1)$. To make this question more concrete, is the reduplicant in *jimgimgan* /img/ or /gim/? This appears to be a no win situation as far as the understanding of reduplication goes from an output goal perspective. If we posit /img/ as the reduplicant, then Prosodic Morphology (McCarthy and Prince 1986) suffers because the reduplicant is the rhyme of one syllable plus the onset of the following syllable and this is not a legitimate prosodic unit. If the other tack is taken by positing /gim/, then the generalization that reduplicants are contiguous strings of segments is lost (/img/ is a contiguous string in *jimgan* but /gim/ is not). Neither of these conclusions is necessary in our new representational approach though.

The pattern of reduplication in Mangarrayi can be accounted for straightforwardly by the present proposals via the precedence variables in (132). Informally, (132) states that the segment preceding the second vowel precedes the first vowel.

(132) a. *begin → end*   b.

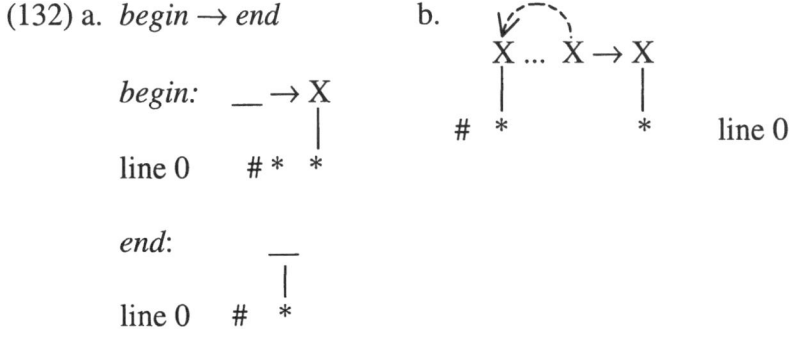

An alternative formulation of (132) could use syllabic information to express the relation that the first onset that follows a syllable precedes the first nucleus. The morphology has access to syllabic information as evidenced by allomorphy patterns sensitive to syllabification (Perlmutter 1998) so either formulation is possible. Which form of (132) is preferred by learners must be left to future research.

The generalization expressed in (132) correctly captures the behavior of reduplication in Mangarrayi as shown in (133).

(133) a. $\# \rightarrow j \rightarrow i \rightarrow m \rightarrow g \rightarrow a \rightarrow n \rightarrow \%$
     b. $\# \rightarrow j \rightarrow i \rightarrow m \rightarrow g \rightarrow a \rightarrow n \rightarrow \%$

     c. $\# \rightarrow j \rightarrow i \rightarrow m \rightarrow g \rightarrow i \rightarrow m \rightarrow g \rightarrow a \rightarrow n \rightarrow \%$

The loop in (133b) is linearized in (133c) to produce the correct surface form. This analysis utilizes the prelinearized metrical structure of the base to capture the complex surface behavior in a simple way. It is the pursuit of a surface true generalization of a contiguous prosodic target that causes Mangarrayi to appear strange. If the output based view of reduplicative templates is abandoned then the deeper generalization relevant to Mangarrayi CVC reduplication as encoded in (132) is discovered.

Previous analyses of Mangarrayi have either had to invoke special mechanisms or they contain conspiracies. In particular, McCarthy and Prince (1986:36-38) invoke extrametricality and prosodic circumscription in order to account for Mangarrayi. Consider the analysis in (134) offered by McCarthy and Prince.

(134) a.   σ   σ
          /|\ /|\
         j i m g a n

     b. σ +   σ   σ
            |\ /|\
        (j) i m g a n

c.
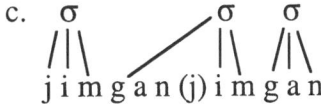

The extrametricality/prosodic circumscription analysis offered by McCarthy and Prince begins in (134a) with the unaffixed base. (134b) shows the affix of the template which also triggers the circumscription of the first vowel of the base. The circumscription is indicated by the /j/ in parentheses and the deletion of the association line between the syllable and this consonant. (134c) shows the association of the copied melody to the syllable template and the additional association of the /g/ from the copied melody to the first syllable of the base so an onset is formed. The derivation is completed by the stray erasure of the non-associated copied melody.

The analysis in (134) implies that reduplication in Mangarrayi is fundamentally different from other types of CVC reduplication because the extra mechanism of prosodic circumscription is required. This point separates the analysis of Mangarrayi from other prosodic morphology analyses of Ilokano or Mokilese because these other CVC reduplication patterns do not require prosodic circumscription. This allows an argument to made in favor of the present analyses since Mangarrayi is accounted for with the same resources as the other CVC reduplication patterns. The only difference between Mangarrayi and Ilokano is the settings of the precedence variables in a readjustment rule. No additional ad hoc mechanism is required.

An alternative analysis of Mangarrayi based in Optimality Theory is offered by Jones (1997). Jones argues that the reduplication pattern in Mangarrayi results from the interaction of generalized alignment constraints that determine the infixation of the reduplicant and relativized CONTIGUITY (McCarthy and Prince 1995) constraints. The main thrust of Jones' analysis is that reduplication in Mangarrayi copies the onset from the following syllable and copies the rime from the preceding syllable.[16] This is the previously discussed C_2VC_1 option for accounting for this reduplication pattern. The important aspect of this analysis is the use of two relativized CONTIGUITY constraints that are presented in (135).

(135) a. J-CONTIGUITY-σ_{IO}: A pair of segments that are adjacent across a syllable boundary in the output are adjacent in the input.

   b. D-CONTIGUITY-σ_{IO}: A pair of segments that are adjacent within a syllable in the output are adjacent in the input.

Given the constraints in (135) and generalized alignment constraints that determine the placement of the reduplicant, the tableau in (136) shows how these constraints interact. Note that ALIGN in (136) is a cover constraint for the two constraints that Jones uses to derive the placement of the reduplicant.

(136)

/jimgan, RED/	ALIGN	J-CONTIGUITY	D-CONTIGUITY
a. jim-**gim**-gan			* (gi)
b. jim-**gam**-gan			* (am)
c. **jim**-jim-gan	*!	* (mj)	
d. jim-**jim**-gan		*! (mj)	
e. jim-**gan**-gan		*! (ng)	
f. jim-**jan**-gan		*!* (mj, ng)	* (ja)
g. jim-**gi**-gan		*! (ig)	* (gi)

The tableau in (136) indicates that the analysis offered by Jones does not produce the correct output form as being most harmonic. Candidates (136a) and (136b) tic in the amount of violations so which of these forms is most harmonic is indeterminate.

   Another problem with the analysis offered by Jones is that forms that show CV reduplication are not accounted for by the proposed relativized CONTIGUITY constraints. Instead, independent relativized LINEARITY (McCarthy and Prince 1995) constraints must be invoked. These LINEARITY constraints are relativized to be sensitive to syllable boundaries in the output as the constraints in (135) are. The difference between CONTIGUITY and LINEARITY is that CONTIGUITY evaluates whether two segments are adjacent to one another regardless of linear order. LINEARITY evaluates whether two segments that are adjacent have the same linear order between them in whatever two levels are being calculated (input/output, base/reduplicant, output/output, etc.) Consider the tableau in (137) which shows the CV reduplication pattern.

(137)

/walima, RED/	J-CONT	J-LINEARITY	D-CONT	D-LINEARITY
☞ a. wa-la-lima				* (la)
b. wa-li-lima		*! (il)		

(137) shows that the relativized CONTIGUITY constraints that account for the CVC reduplication pattern in Mangarrayi are insufficient to account for the forms that undergo CV reduplication. Neither candidate in (137) violates either CONTIGUITY constraint. In addition, the added LINEARITY constraints do not help in solving the indeterminacy seen in tableau (136) because the tied candidates both violate D-LINEARITY to the same extent. Because of the different explanations provided for the CVC and CV reduplication patterns we can conclude that Jones' analysis is conspiratorial in nature. CONTIGUITY and LINEARITY conspire in this Optimality Theory analysis to produce the overall pattern of reduplication in Mangarrayi. From this we can argue that the analysis of Mangarrayi presented here is superior to the one in Jones (1997) because this analysis provides a single generalization based on where a precedence link should be added that accounts for both CVC and CV reduplicants in Mangarrayi. These different patterns in reduplication result from whether there is a consonant cluster between the first and second vowels in the base that the precedence link described in (132) concatenates to. Furthermore, according to this analysis Mangarrayi behaves like all the other reduplication patterns presented so far in that the precedence variables that are present in the phonological representation of a morpheme determine the surface effect of the added precedence link. The pattern of reduplication in Mangarrayi is unusual only in that it appears to invoke a rarer and more complex combination of precedence variables than other reduplication patterns in the literature.

3.4.4 ONSET and NOCODA effects

One argument frequently presented in favor of the Optimality Theory model of reduplication is the emergence of the unmarked
(McCarthy and Prince 1994a) effects found in some reduplication
patterns. Two of the most well know effects are the ONSET effect
and the NOCODA effect. Both of these patterns are easily accounted
for in the present proposals without resorting to output based prosodic targets.

The ONSET effect pattern of reduplication is typically total reduplication with the omission of a word initial vowel. In these special
cases the entire root except the initial vowel reduplicates. This effect can also occur with partial reduplication but the example that
will be analyzed coincides with the description given above.

Optimality Theory analyses explain the ONSET effect as the
ranking of ONSET above MAX_{BR}. This effect can be reinterpreted as
an edge effect given the present proposals instead of the output oriented prosodic well-formedness approach provided by Optimality
Theory.

ONSET effects can be produced by setting the ending precedence
variable of a morpheme to "first onset". This setting can be
achieved through reference to syllabification information. Alternatively, the first onset can also be identified as the first consonant
that precedes a vowel. The notion first is derived by allowing the
precedence variables to search through the precedence structure that
they will concatenate to from beginning (#) to end (%). First is immediately derived by stopping this search and concatenating as
soon as the structural description of the precedence variable is met.
A segmental description of the precedence variable settings that
will produce an ONSET effect is in (138).

(138) a. *begin → end*   b.

$$
\begin{array}{ll}
begin: & \_\_ \to \% \\
end: & \_\_ \quad \to \quad X \\
& [Cplace] \\
& \quad\quad | \\
& \quad * \quad \text{line 0}
\end{array}
$$

b.

$$
\#\dots X \quad \to X \dots X \to \% \\
[Cplace] \quad\quad | \\
\quad\quad\quad\quad * \text{ line 0}
$$

(138) states that the ending precedence variable is the first consonant that precedes a vowel. For consonant initial forms this will be equivalent to the word initial segment and for vowel initial forms it will be some word internal segment. The alternative approach to defining the precedence variables mentioned earlier that utilizes the notion onset would be required for languages that can have complex onsets. The present formulation of (138) will work for languages that only allow simplex onsets.

A concrete example of this phenomenon can be seen in Axininca Campa (McCarthy and Prince 1993b, 1994a). The relevant data is presented in (139).

(139) kawosi   kawosi-kawosi   'paddle'
　　　 osampi   osampi-sampi   'ask'

This pattern of reduplication in Axininca Campa reduplicates the entire word except for a word initial vowel. (138) correctly models this effect as seen in the derivation in (140).

(140) a. $\# \rightarrow o \rightarrow s \rightarrow a \rightarrow m \rightarrow p \rightarrow i \rightarrow \%$

　　　 b. $\# \rightarrow o \rightarrow s \rightarrow a \rightarrow m \rightarrow p \rightarrow i \rightarrow \%$

Since (138) specifies an ending precedence variable that may occur in different absolute positions in a precedence structure, a natural edge-based analysis of ONSET effects results from the present proposals. As with the analysis of CVC reduplication in the previous section, the analysis here does not invoke the idea of output targets at all and derives the ONSET effect directly through the specification of precedence variables. For an analysis and discussion of the back-copying augmentation facts in Axininca Campa based on the present proposals see Frampton (1999).

The other highly touted emergence of the unmarked effect in the Optimality Theory literature is the NOCODA effect. This effect also results from an emergence of the unmarked ranking where NO CODA is ranked above MAX_{BR} but below input output faithfulness.

This causes the last consonant in a reduplicant to not be copied if it is a coda. Consider the example from Balangao (McCarthy and Prince 1994b) in (141). Note that "R" represents the placement of RED in (141).

(141) ma-R-taynan   ma-tayna-taynan 'repeatedly be left behind'
      ka-R-?abulot   ka-?abu-?abulot 'believers of just everything'

The pertinent facts about Balangao reduplication is that two syllables of material equaling a foot are reduplicated from the stem and that prefixes are ignored in reduplication. This fact can be derived from either having the prefixes in question directly trigger the application of a readjustment rule producing reduplication or by having a zero morph that triggers reduplication affixed to the stem prior to the prefixes. The NOCODA effect in this type of reduplication is the lack of constituent copying that is seen. Reduplication here does not copy whole syllables (this would predict that /ma-RED-taynan/ would reduplicate as *ma-taynan-taynan*) but instead it only copies up to the second vowel in the stem. As previously mentioned, Optimality Theory proposes that this effect is due to NOCODA which penalizes the reduplication of coda segments.

   An edge based analysis that is parallel to the one given for ONSET effects is available though. This NOCODA effect is the result of setting the beginning precedence variable of the reduplicative morpheme to a vowel. The particular foot reduplication in Balangao can be represented as in (142).

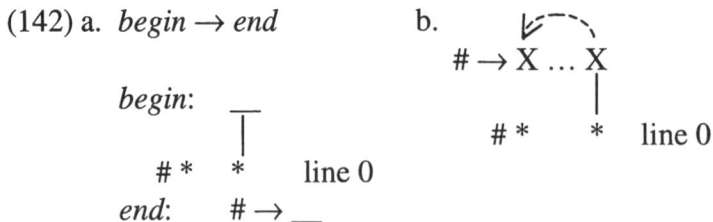

Since the beginning environment of the readjustment rule in (142) only refers to elements of the metrical grid it will ignore consonants (since they do not project onto the grid) and anchor onto the second vowel of the phonological representation. The second vowel can be identified either through foot structure already present in the form or by a separate footing of the form triggered by this morpheme. (143) provides a derivation to show how the readjustment rule in (142) derives the forms in (141).

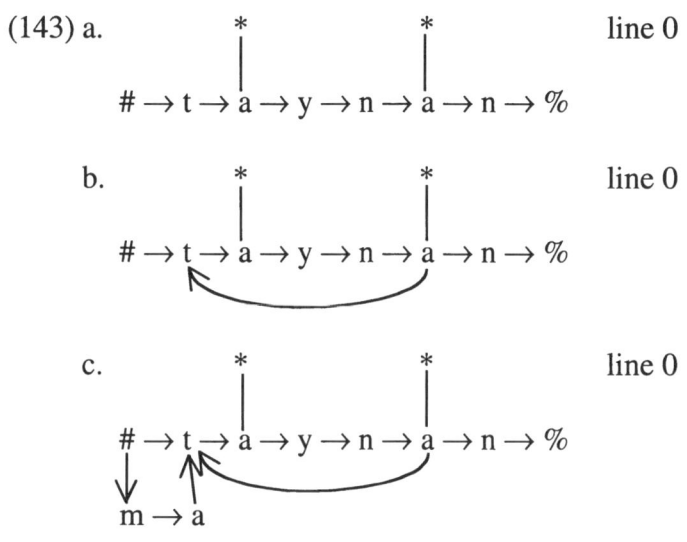

(143) a.   *   *   line 0

     # → t → a → y → n → a → n → %

   b.   *   *   line 0

     # → t → a → y → n → a → n → %

   c.   *   *   line 0

     # → t → a → y → n → a → n → %

     m → a

   d. #mataynataynan%

While this edge based representational approach to NoCODA effects captures the same generalization as an Optimality Theory based account, it does not make the same predictions. Stemberger (1996) points out that the Optimality Theory NoCODA analysis predicts that *all* codas in a reduplicant could be stripped out by this constraint (thus *tagtag* would reduplicate as *tata-tagtag*) in a very easy and natural way (No CODA >> MAX$_{BR}$, CONTIGUITY). Consider the tableau in (144).

(144)

RED+tagtagtag	No CODA	MAX$_{BR}$	CONTIGUITY
a. tagtagtag-tagtagtag	****!**		
b. tagtagta-tagtagtag	****!*	*	
☞ c. tatata-tagtagtag	***	***	**

As can be seen in (144), candidate (144c) which eliminates all co-das in the reduplicant is the winner. This candidate is the most har-monic with respect to NoCODA so it is optimal given this particular constraint ranking. This is an unattested pattern of reduplication and consequently the Optimality Theory model of reduplication must adopt an ad hoc stipulation mandating the ranking of CONTIGUITY >> NoCODA to prevent this pattern from occurring. The analysis proposed here does not suffer from this overgeneration of patho-logical reduplication patterns since it treats this phenomenon as an edge-based effect.

The attested NoCODA pattern is produced in the present propos-als by setting the ending precedence variable in a readjustment rule to concatenate only to a vowel. For a hypothetical total reduplica-tion pattern that shows a NoCODA effect, the graph in (145) would be created.

(145) $\# \rightarrow t \rightarrow a \rightarrow g \rightarrow t \rightarrow a \rightarrow g \rightarrow t \rightarrow a \rightarrow g \rightarrow \%$

The crucial aspect of this example is that the readjustment rule in question only adds a single precedence link. Since only a single link is added, only a single coda is skipped. A graph that would produce pathological NoCODA effects is found in (146).

(146)
$\# \rightarrow t \rightarrow a \rightarrow g \rightarrow t \rightarrow a \rightarrow g \rightarrow t \rightarrow a \rightarrow g \rightarrow \%$

To construct the graph in (146) an additional link must be added for each coda that is to be skipped. This variability in the number of links being added to a stem depending on what the base is prevents this type of pattern from being the result of a productive rule.

The argument that pathological NoCODA effects cannot be a productive process in the present proposals can be derived from ar-guments in Carrier (1979) and McCarthy and Prince (1986) against using CV templates to describe reduplication patterns. CV tem-plates are unable to account for total reduplication because of the variable nature of total reduplication. Since it is possible that every stem that undergoes total reduplication could require a different configuration of Cs and Vs, Carrier and McCarthy and Prince argue that CV templates are unable to capture the core generalization of total reduplication. This argument holds for the present proposals in productively creating pathological NOCODA effects. Since the amount of "jump links" needed to eliminate all codas in the reduplicant will vary from stem to stem, there is no productive generalization that can be made. This indicates that the non-output based approach to NOCODA effects proposed here is more restrictive than the output based Optimality Theory approach. In part, it cannot generate pathological NOCODA effects.

3.4.5 Atemplatic reduplication

The final type of reduplication pattern to be presented here that provides evidence for the proposals in this chapter is referred to as atemplatic reduplication. Both Gafos (1998a) and Hendricks (1998) make the claim that Temiar and Semai present evidence of a reduplicant that is not a legitimate prosodic unit. The reduplicant in these languages is a product of other forces in the grammars of these languages.

Gafos (1998a) points out that the Prosodic Morphology hypothesis only requires templates to be made of legitimate prosodic units and does not require all reduplication to be templatic but this is a new interpretation or view of reduplication. Previously, attempts were made to account for both Semai and Temiar in templatic ways (Shaw 1993, Sloan 1988) through the positing of minor syllables as prosodic units. This view makes a much stronger claim about the nature of reduplication in that it retains the idea that all reduplication patterns are subject to the same restrictions.

The strong view about constraining all types of reduplication is retained in the model of reduplication proposed here. As proposed in the analysis of Nancowry in section 3.3, a discontiguous reduplication pattern can be produced by positing morphemes with more than two precedence variables. Consider the data from Semai (Diffolth 1976) in (147) and Temiar[17] (Benjamin 1976) in (148). The pattern of reduplication for both languages indicates continuative aspect.

(147) dŋɔh   dh-dŋɔh   'appearance of nodding'
      cʔɛ:t   ct-cʔɛ:t   'sweet'
      bʔəl   bl-bʔəl   'painful embarrassment'
      ghʉp   gp-ghʉp   'irritation on skin'
      kmrʔɛ:c   kc-kmrʔɛ:c   'short, fat arms'

(148) a. slɔg   s-g-lɔg   'to sleep with'
         smãɲ   s-ɲ-mãɲ   'to ask a question'

      b. kɔ̄w   kw-kɔ̄w   'to call'
         gəl   gl-gəl   'to sit down'
         rec   rɲ-rec   'to eat'

The difference between the reduplication patterns in Temiar and Semai is a very subtle one. Semai reduplicates and prefixes the first and last segments as seen in (147). Temiar presents a more complicated pattern where forms with three consonants, (148a), reduplicate the final segment and infix it after the first consonant while forms in (148b) with only two consonants reduplicate the first and last consonant and prefix them. Thus, Temiar forms with two consonants follow the same pattern as Semai does but Temiar forms with three consonants do not.

The Semai pattern of reduplication can be produced by the precedence variables in (149).

(149) a. *begin* → *mid* → *end*   b. $\# \to X \ldots X \to \%$

         begin: # → __

         mid: __ → %

         end: # → __

The precedence structure described in (149) is that the first segment precedes the last segment which precedes the first segment. Adding this precedence structure to one of the bases in (147) creates a precedence structure as seen in (150).

(150) a.

$$\# \to k \to m \to r \to \text{?} \to \text{ə:} \to c \to \%$$

b. $\# \to k \to c \to k \to m \to r \to \text{?} \to \text{ə:} \to c \to \%$

The precedence structure in (150a) is linearized as (150b) because the added precedence link from the word initial segment to the word final segment is followed first since it is new information when compared with the competing [k → m] link. Since this precedence link contains three precedence variables there is no choice at the word final segment. Since the ending variable is part of the precedence link started by following the [k → c] link in (150a), the [c →k] must be followed immediately. At the word initial segment again, linearization proceeds by going straight through the remaining lexical links.

The reduplication pattern in Temiar can be produced by modifying one of the precedence variables in (149). This is a very important finding because the close relation between Temiar and Semai is reflected in the similarity of the morphemes that produce their reduplication patterns. The modification that must be made to the precedence structure in (149) in order to produce the Temiar pattern is presented in (151).

(151) a. *begin* → *mid* → *end*   b.

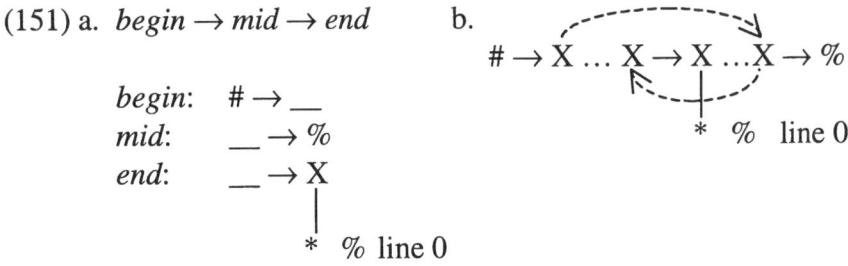

begin: # → __
mid: __ → %
end: __ → X

The precedence structure that is described in (151) specifies that the first segment precedes the last segment which precedes the segment that precedes the last vowel. This last precedence variable is similar to the one used to produce NoCODA effects in the analysis of Balangao in section 3.4.4. The difference between the precedence variable used here and the one required in Balangao is that Temiar identifies the last vowel and Balangao specifies a vowel at the end of a foot (in other words, the second vowel).

Whether the ending precedence variable in (151) makes reference to the segment that precedes the last vowel or first onset depends on what the status of minor syllables are in Temiar. All analyses of Temiar (Benjamin 1976, McCarthy 1982, Broselow and McCarthy 1983, Sloan 1988, Shaw 1993, Gafos 1998ab) assume the existence of minor syllables in Temiar. Both Sloan (1988) and Shaw (1993) specifically address the prosodic status of minor syllables. All of these views of minor syllables assume that prosodic licensing (Ito 1988) requires segments to be parsed into syllables if they are present in the output. Bagemihl (1989) convincingly argues that Bella Coola has unsyllabified segments and this allows minor syllables to be understood as phonologically unsyllabified segments. Phonetic descriptions of minor syllables indicate that there is usually a short vowel of variable quality that acts as some kind of nucleus in these syllables. This fact supports the view that minor syllables are phonologically unsyllabified segments because the phonetics module can either add vowels to these unsyllabified segments or these variable vowels can be produced by the transition of articulatory gestures between the two consonants.

While the status of minor syllables is important in determining what the best analysis of Temiar is they do not affect the ability of the present proposals in accounting for the data. The formulation of (151) takes a neutral position on the status of minor syllables and derives the reduplication patterns using a different reference point. (152) presents the precedence structures resulting from the concatenation of (152) with both a three consonant and two consonant root.

(152) a.

$$\# \rightarrow s \rightarrow l \rightarrow \mathfrak{d} \rightarrow g \rightarrow \%$$

b.
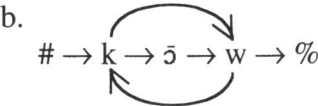
$\# \rightarrow k \rightarrow \tilde{\mathfrak{I}} \rightarrow w \rightarrow \%$

The precedence structures in (152) show how different prosodic structures of individual words can produce different reduplication patterns even though the same precedence structure is added. In (152a), there is a distinction between the first segment of the precedence structure and the segment that precedes the last vowel and this produces the single infixed consonant reduplication pattern in Temiar. (152b) shows the Semai like reduplication pattern where the first and last segment are reduplicated and prefixed results when the first segment of the precedence graph and the segment that precedes the last vowel are the same segment. Variation in a reduplication pattern emerging from differences in the stems that a precedence structure is added to is also seen in the previous Mangarrayi example.

The analyses of Temiar and Semai presented here provide support for the present proposals for two main reasons. The first is that the similarity between (149) and (151) directly captures the close relationship between the reduplication patterns in Temiar and Semai. The Optimality Theory analyses offered by Gafos (1998a) and Hendricks (1998) are significantly different from each other and do not capture this generalization. Gafos claims that reduplication in Temiar results from the interaction of requiring the reduplicant to be next to a stressed syllable, which is always final in Temiar (Benjamin 1976), and an onset requirement. Hendricks claims that reduplication in Semai results from the interaction of the requirement of anchoring both ends of the reduplicant while reduplicating as little segmental material as possible. It is not clear how these two analyses relate the reduplication patterns in Temiar and Semai with each other nor is it clear how to derive one analysis from the other.

The second reason that the present analysis should be preferred is that non-prosodic discontinuous reduplication patterns do not force the present model of reduplication to be modified in any way. Patterns of reduplication result from the precedence structures that are described by precedence variables and more complicated reduplication patterns result from precedence variables utilizing more complicated descriptions of points in a precedence graph or by using additional precedence variables. Both of these options are inherent properties of the model of reduplication developed here. Consequently, the fact that more complicated reduplication patterns match up with more complicated precedence variables is a strong argument in favor of the present proposals.

4.5   Summary

This chapter has addressed the morphological issues raised by the representations proposed in chapter 2. In addition, the basic process of morpheme concatenation has been addressed. All issues related to reduplicative templates and the morphology of reduplication have been given a unified approach within Distributed Morphology. This supports the claim that reduplication and associated phenomena can be accounted for within a modular and derivational theory of morphology and phonology.

The analyses presented in this chapter call into question some of the basic findings and tenets of Optimality Theory. All instances of emergence of the unmarked effects in reduplication have been given simple rule based analyses here. There is no need for parallel computation or correspondence to produce any of these types of effects. The analyses presented here have been shown to be superior to the analyses of the languages used to argue for the emergence of the unmarked, therefore analyses of reduplication dependent on the emergence of the unmarked must be reevaluated and reargued to address the issues raised here.

Another argument in favor of the proposals in this chapter is based on the idea that formal markedness and analytic simplicity should coincide. The idea behind this argument is that the formal systems that are proposed in linguistic theory should reflect in some way what is marked in human language. Additionally, the formal system should indicate and predict what operations are more complicated than others. With the advent of linguistics becoming an active part of cognitive science in general, we must hold our formal systems to these goals. A formal system that does not make the correct predictions in respect to what is complex or should cause processing or acquisition difficulties is inferior to one that makes the correct predictions.

The model of reduplication proposed here has the characteristic that it makes predictions about which reduplication patterns are more marked than others. These predictions are based on the idea of analytic simplicity in that patterns that require fewer or less complicated precedence variables are simpler and thus less marked. Patterns that require complex precedence variables or additional precedence variables are more marked. The analyses of reduplicative templates presented in section 3.4 have this quality.

The nature of the precedence structures gives special status to both the beginning and end of forms. Consequently total reduplication results from the most basic combination of precedence variables. The simplicity of this precedence structure makes the prediction that total reduplication is the least marked type of reduplication. This prediction is true. Almost every language in the world has total reduplication of some sort (Moravcsik 1978).

Following from this point, all other patterns of reduplication should be formally marked. ONSET and NOCODA effects in reduplication patterns are more complicated because of the reference either to only consonants or vowels in one of the precedence variables. Patterns of partial reduplication (e.g. Tohono O'odham, Ilokano) require more complicated environments in at least one of the precedence variables. Infixing patterns of reduplication (e.g. Mangarrayi) require both precedence variables to be more complicated than just "beginning" or "end". Discontiguous reduplication patterns (e.g. Temiar, Semai) require three precedence variables to produce the correct pattern of reduplication. Combinations of different types of reduplication effects such as partial infixed ONSET effect patterns are even more marked due to the combination of the individual complexity of each effect. Finally, the apparent unmarkedness of prefixing reduplication can be derived in the present system through a preference for reference to the beginning of a lexical item $[\# \rightarrow \_\_]$ which agrees with various psycholinguistics findings.

The natural incorporation of a markedness metric is only one advantage of the present model of reduplication. The final chapter will discuss other advantages of the present approach by identifying strengths and weaknesses in previous approaches to reduplication.

Chapter 4
Theoretical issues and conclusion

One of the primary purposes of this book has been to argue for a formal clarification of the representations used in phonological theory in which precedence relationships are explicitly specified. A trivial but striking argument that shows the need for precedence in phonological representations is the simple fact that *ab* and *ba* are distinguished in all of the world's languages. There are no "anagram" languages. This results from precedence being a primitive in phonological representations.

The arguments presented here in favor of the explicit representation of precedence are a bit more complicated though. Primarily, these arguments use reduplication to show the benefits of the explicit representation of precedence. From the formal representation of precedence a new representationally based model of reduplication has been developed. Comparisons of this new model of reduplication with previous models of reduplication across many different dimensions provide numerous arguments for this new model of reduplication and the explicit representation of precedence. Additionally, we have found evidence from infixes that further support the proposals about precedence in chapters 2 and 3.

This final chapter presents three more general arguments in favor of the model of reduplication developed here. These arguments address theoretical issues affecting phonological theory and indicate what role reduplication has in illuminating possible theories of phonology. The answers to these theoretical issues provided by the present model of reduplication are an improvement on the answers from previous models of reduplication. This kind of converging reduplication independent evidence is one of the strongest arguments in favor of the proposals in this book. Finally, other topics in phonology and morphology that may benefit from the proposals in this book will be identified.

4.1   Conspiracies

One of the advantages Optimality Theory analyses claim over rule based analyses is in the area of conspiracies. Since Optimality Theory prefers to make generalizations on surface forms and eschews intermediate representations, conspiracies based on putative output goals should not occur. Conspiracies should not occur in Optimality Theory because a direct surface generalization can be made which should eliminate redundancies present in non-surface true generalizations that are the usual source of conspiracies. As indicated by the discussion of CVC reduplication in Mangarrayi in chapter 3, Optimality Theory analyses are still capable of containing conspiracies and the analysis of Mangarrayi presented by Jones (1997) is one concrete example. Consider the constraints and ranking that Jones requires to account for the Mangarrayi reduplication pattern presented in (153).

(153)   J-CONTIGUITY-σ_{IO} >>   D-CONTIGUITY-σ_{IO}
         J-LINEARITY-σ_{IO} D-LINEARITY-σ_{IO}

There is a certain amount of overlap between CONTIGUITY and LINEARITY that causes Jones' analysis to contain a conspiracy. Neither CONTIGUITY nor LINEARITY alone is sufficient to account for the entire reduplication pattern in Mangarrayi. The relativized CONTIGUITY constraints account for the CVC pattern of reduplication and the relativized LINEARITY constraints account for the CV pattern of reduplication. The analysis based on the model of reduplication developed here makes a single generalization that covers the behavior of both patterns of reduplication. Consequently, since we have an alternative to compare the Jones (1997) Optimality Theory analysis with, we can identify the conspiratorial nature of Jones' analysis. See Halle and Idsardi (to appear) for a discussion of the conspiracies present in Optimality Theory analyses of metrical systems.

Since it is apparent that conspiracies can plague all theories, both classical generative phonology and Optimality Theory in the present discussion, no simple argument based on conspiracies can be made in favor of either model of phonology. More detailed and language specific arguments based on conspiracies must be offered instead. An outline with examples of three different types of arguments based on conspiracies that can be used to distinguish between different analyses follows.

The first type of argument from conspiracies that can be made is the *classic conspiracy argument*. The form of such an argument is that an analysis misses a generalization when there is no single coherent expression of it. We favor analyses that capture more generalizations. Consequently, we should pick an analysis that captures more generalizations. This type of argument was used to distinguish between the Jones (1997) analysis of Mangarrayi and the analysis presented here.

This type of conspiracy argument can also be brought against the Optimality Theory approach to templates in reduplication. The point that is being raised here is that neither the direct expression of a template (such as RED = $\sigma_{\mu\mu}$) nor the more recent innovation of deriving a template from constraint interaction that is assumed by *generalized template theory* (McCarthy and Prince 1994b) addresses how the template is satisfied. The "template" in these cases only indicates an output structure and other constraints must be invoked to indicate where the template should occur in the output, what correspondences between the base and reduplicant are permissible in the template, and finally under what conditions and along which dimensions the "template" can be violated. When all of these other issues are considered it becomes apparent that a template under any interpretation provides very little information about a reduplication pattern. Since only a small amount of information is provided by a template, only a vague generalization can be made by this device. Any generalization that is posited by a "template" would be further weakened if the "template" itself is not a generalization but instead is composed out of other entities as in the generalized template theory (McCarthy and Prince 1994b) approach.

To illustrate the dispersement of the aspects of a reduplication pattern in an Optimality Theory analysis consider the tableau in (154). This tableau shows the constraints that must be involved and crucial candidates that must be considered in order to account for the prefixing heavy syllable reduplication pattern in Ilokano (Hayes and Abad 1989). The particular form that will be analyzed in the tableau in (154) is *kal-kaldíŋ* 'goats' from *kaldíŋ* 'goat' and we will ignore how stress and reduplication interact.

(154)

/RED, kaldiŋ/	RED=σ$_{μμ}$	PREFIX	ANCH	CONTIG	FAITH	MARK
☞ a. kal-kaldiŋ				*	*...	*+...
b. ka-kaldiŋ	*!				*+...	*+...
c. kaa-kaldiŋ				*+!	*+...	*+...
d. kaldiŋ-kaldiŋ	*!			*		*+...
e. kaldiŋ-kaldiŋ	*!	*		*		*+...
f. kaldiŋ-diŋ		*!	*	*	*...	*+...
g. diŋ-kaldiŋ			*!	*	*-...	*+...
h. kaŋ-kaldiŋ				*+!	*-...	*+...
i. ʔən-kaldiŋ			*!	*+	*+...	*-...
j. ʔal-kaldiŋ				*	*+...	*-...
k. dil-kaldiŋ			*!	*+	*+...	*+...
l. kal-kadiŋ				*+!	*?...	*-...

The constraints in (154) are not actual constraints but instead are shorthand for particular rankings of specific constraints. Each of these cover constraints will be discussed in turn to show the inter-action of the specific constraints.

The first constraint in (154) is RED = σ$_{μμ}$ and is composed of at least REALIZE MORPHEME and an alignment constraint if generalized template theory is assumed. REALIZE MORPHEME requires RED to correspond with some segmental material in the output. UNIFORMITY (McCarthy and Prince 1995) which prevents multiple correspondence will also be active to ensure that RED and the base do not correspond to the same segmental material in the output resulting in no repetition of phonological material. Both of these constraints must be ranked above *STRUCT, which penalizes all segmental material, otherwise there would be no surface difference in a form triggered by RED.

The alignment constraint component of RED = σ$_{μμ}$ will require RED to be right aligned with a heavy syllable but there are some complications to this approach. If this alignment constraint simply requires RED to be right aligned with a heavy syllable then it is equivalent to a template because a direct structural requirement is placed on RED. This is contradictory to the spirit of generalized template theory[1] (McCarthy and Prince 1994b). Other options for this alignment constraint lead to either analytic indeterminacy because the alignment target does not distinguish between a heavy and light syllable (as in the case of right aligning to a mora) or to the further fractioning of constraints. This fractioning of the constraint results from the Ilokano reduplication pattern lengthening short vowels to meet the heavy syllable "template" (as in *ró?ot* > *roo-ró?ot* 'leaves [plural]') which causes both "right-align with a C" and "right-align with a long vowel" to be inadequate in describing the total pattern in Ilokano. I leave the issue of whether generalized template theory can derive heavy syllable reduplication patterns without positing a de facto template to future research.

It can now be seen that the cover constraint RED = $\sigma_{\mu\mu}$ actually involves at least the constraints and ranking in (155).

(155) REALIZE MORPHEME
     UNIFORMITY   >>   *STRUCT
     ALIGN (R, RED, R, $\sigma_{\mu\mu}$)

The candidates that violate this cover constraint all either copy too much material as in candidates (154d,e) or copy too little material as in candidate (154b). None of these candidates contain a reduplicant that is coextensive with a heavy syllable.

The PREFIX cover constraint in (154) indicates that an alignment constraint that requires the right edge of RED to be aligned with the left edge of the stem is ranked higher than other competing alignment constraints. The competing alignment constraints are ones that require RED to align with the right edge of the stem (producing suffixing reduplication) or some kind of infixing or variable placement (as in align to the left of the main stressed syllable) of RED. For any type of reduplication pattern, the alignment constraint (or constraints in some cases) that correctly describes the placement of RED in the output must dominate all other alignment constraints that require RED to align in some other way. This produces the constraint ranking in (156) for the prefix cover constraint.

(156) ALIGN (R, RED, L, Stem) >> ALIGN (L, RED, R, Stem)
                     ALIGN X

The candidates in (154) that violate this cover constraint all show suffixing reduplication. Candidate (154e) shows total reduplication with the second part being the reduplicant and candidate (154f) also shows suffixing (or possibly infixing) reduplication and neither of these options satisfy the prefix cover constraint.

The ANCH cover constraint refers to ANCHOR constraints (McCarthy and Prince 1995) that require the beginning or end of the reduplicant to correspond with the beginning or end of the base. This particular pattern of reduplication requires ANCHOR-Left which states that the left most segment in the reduplicant correspond with the left most segment in the base to be ranked above ANCHOR-Right which places the opposite requirement on RED. This results in the ranking in (157) for the ANCH cover constraint.

(157) ANCHOR-Left >> ANCHOR-Right

The candidates that violate this cover constraint all begin the reduplicant with a segment other than the leftmost segment in the base. Candidates (154g,k) begin the reduplicant with /d/ which is in the middle of the base.[2] Candidate (154i) shows a default RED where the segmental content of RED are epenthetic segments that do not correspond with the segments in the base. Candidate (154j) satisfies ANCH because the initial segment, /ʔ/, corresponds to /k/ in the base but has been modified to reduce markedness (as in the Alderete et al 1999 analysis of prespecification in reduplication).

The CONTIG cover constraint refers to the different possible ranking of CONTIGUITY constraints. Most candidates in (154) violate CONTIGUITY to a certain extent since there is the sequence of segments between the reduplicant and the base that is not contained in the input.[3] The single candidate that does not have this violation is candidate (154b) because /a/ and /k/ are contiguous in the input. Relative severeness of violations of CONTIGUITY are indicated in (154) by a "+" or "-" that indicates whether the candidate is more or less harmonic with respect to CONTIGUITY than the winning candidate in (154a). Candidates that are eliminated by this cover constraint are (154c) which will have an additional violation caused by the epenthetic /a/ and the segments that border it in the output, (154h) which has the additional sequence of [aŋ], and (154l) that contains [ad] as a sequence in the base which is not present in the input. The ranking of specific contiguity constraints in this cover constraint is in (158).

(158) CONTIGUITY$_{IO}$ >>   J-CONTIGUITY$_{IO}$, D-CONTIGUITY$_{IO}$, etc.

The ranking in (158) indicates that the more general input/output CONTIGUITY constraint will be ranked above other more specific CONTIGUITY constraints in this particular type of reduplication pattern.

The FAITH cover constraint refers to all the Faithfulness constraints that require exact copying between the base and reduplicant. Additionally, the Faithfulness constraints that affect only the base are included here also. As with the CONTIG cover constraint, relative violations of this set of constraints is indicated in (154). The candidates in (154d,e) that show total reduplication are more harmonic along the Faithfulness dimension than the winning candidate in (154a). The candidate that is eliminated by this constraint is (154j) which has miscopied /k/ as /ʔ/ in the reduplicant in an attempt to reduce markedness.

The MARK cover constraint refers to all Markedness constraints. Because of the particular ranking in (154), MARK does not help determine the winning candidate but we can still see how MARK could affect the determination of the surface reduplication pattern. As before, relative violations of MARK are indicated by + or - symbols to show whether a candidate is more or less harmonic than the winning candidate in (154a). Most of the candidates are roughly equivalent to the winning candidate along the dimension of markedness if only number of segments is considered. The total reduplication candidates in (154d,e) show more violations of MARK since more segmental material is reduplicated. Candidate (154b) shows less violations of MARK since only /ka/ is added as the reduplicant. Candidate (154l) also shows less violations of MARK since the /l/ is not present in the base but is present in the reduplicant. Finally, candidates (154i,j) reduce markedness violations along the featural dimension by miscopying in reduplication.

All Optimality Theory analyses of reduplication must at least assume all of the dimensions of variance in a reduplication pattern are accounted for by the sets of constraints and constraint rankings discussed above. From this point, it can be seen that the actual RED $= \sigma_{\mu\mu}$ constraint only accounts for a small portion of the heavy syllable reduplication pattern in Ilokano. This constraint does not have anything to say about where the reduplicant is positioned, how to fill the reduplicant with segmental material, or when the reduplicant may not be a heavy syllable. It is the entire ranking of all the constraints that evaluate a reduplication structure that accounts for the reduplication pattern and this makes it unclear as to what generalization is provided by a single constraint that affects some dimension of reduplication. Due to this fact, Optimality Theory analyses of reduplication are open to conspiracy arguments since the generalization accounting for the pattern does not result from a single statement in the grammar. Instead, generalizations with respect to reduplication in Optimality Theory analyses are provided by the entire grammar of a given language.

When we compare this situation with the analysis of Ilokano provided in section 3.4.3, we see that the analysis presented here provides a single strong generalization (albeit complex) about the reduplication pattern that is encapsulated in a single readjustment rule in the morphology. This readjustment rule, (125/126), determines the placement of the reduplicant, what segmental material is present in the reduplicant, and what variation occurs in the reduplicant. The first two of these points are actually one and the same since there is no copying of melody in this model of reduplication and the placement and what segmental material occurs in the reduplicant are directly dependent on the precedence variables in this readjustment rule. The point here is that arguments based on conspiracies used against rule based analyses can also be raised against Optimality Theory approaches. The line between "constraint interaction" and "constraint conspiracy" appears to be a fine one and its position has not been fully identified yet. Consequently, conspiracies do not uniformly argue for a single model of grammar over other possible models.

The second type of response to conspiracy arguments is the *false conspiracy* argument. This type of argument indicates that what appears at the surface to be a conspiracy is in actuality not. To see how this works, we can again turn to heavy syllable reduplication in Ilokano.

Disregarding the discussion of the classic conspiracy argument, one immediate response to the analysis of Ilokano provided in chapter 3 is that it misses the generalization that the reduplicant is always a heavy syllable. According to this objection, the notion of heavy syllable is meant to capture the lengthening behavior in stems that do not show CVC reduplication. The analysis in chapter 3 instead explains the lengthening behavior of these stems by the presence of an empty X-slot in the precedence links that are added. The evidence that supports this view of heavy syllable reduplication is the fact that Kusaiean (Lee 1975) instantiates the case where CVC and CVV stems differ in reduplicants with no lengthening of the copied vowels in the CVV stems. This fact supports the bi-clausal nature of the reduplication rule in (125/126) because the alternation in reduplication patterns between CVC and CVV stems seen in both Mokilese and Kusaiean is independent of whether a heavy syllable is the surface result of reduplication. To further support this point, the fact that Mokilese appears to be simplifying its heavy syllable reduplication rule to only have the general clause in (130b) to produce a uniform pattern of reduplication that lengthens the reduplicated vowel indicates that a biclausal description of this pattern is correct (see Raimy to appear). In summary, upon deeper investigation of heavy syllable reduplication in Ilokano and Mokilese it turns out that "heavy syllable" is a spurious generalization because it does not capture the cross linguistic typological facts. Consequently, a conspiracy argument can not be made against the analysis of Ilokano in chapter 3 since the supposed missed generalization (heavy syllable) is incorrect.[4]

The final possible type of conspiracy argument is based on a re-interpretation of what a phonological rule is. Avery and Idsardi (to appear) propose that phonological rules can be interpreted as statements about what a representation should be. The effect of this interpretation of phonological rules is that if a structure described as the output of a phonological rule is already present, then the rule will not add any structure since it is satisfied by the presence of this structure. This position allows the analysis of Tohono O'odham in section 3.4.2 to be expanded to explain forms that do not undergo reduplication. Consider the data in (159). The important aspect is to notice is that each of the forms appears to be the result of the readjustment rules proposed to account for reduplication in Tohono O'odham.

(159) a. ʔiʔis   'a plant'
         čučul   'chicken'
         hahaw   'a lung'
         kakaiču   'a quail'

      b. ʔaaʔat   'the dessert'
         giigiwakam   'a winner'
         haahag   'a leaf'
         tiitili   'a talking doll'

      c. gagka   'a clearing'
         kaksipul   'the bells on ...'
         kokʔoi   'a ghost'
         paplo   'a pigeon'

      d. biibhiag   'the morning'
         čuučpul   'a square'
         ʃuuʃk   'a pair of shoes'
         taatko   'a jaw'

The forms in (159a) appear to have under gone CV reduplication since the beginning of the stem has repetitive sequence of CV. The forms in (159b) appear to have undergone CV reduplication and the additional readjustment of long vowel which causes the vowel in the reduplicant to be long. The forms in (159c) appear to have undergone CV reduplication and the jump link readjustment and finally the forms in (159d) appear to have undergone CV reduplication, long vowel readjustment and jump link readjustment.

The lack of reduplication shown by these forms is immediately accounted for by the new interpretation of what a rule is proposed by Avery and Idsardi (to appear). If the appropriate readjustments are "applied" to these forms, the structure that is to be added via the readjustment rule is already present so the rule does not alter the phonological structure further. These forms do not have a distinct reduplicated form since they appear to already have a reduplicated structure. By reinterpreting what kind of operation a rule is, a new approach to accounting for surface targets emerges which helps explain conspiracies. This view may also provide new ideas that may be helpful in understanding haplology effects.

To summarize this section, three points have been made. The first is that conspiracies can affect any theoretical framework so Optimality Theory is not immune from conspiracy arguments. The second is that present Optimality Theory analyses of reduplication patterns are more conspiratorial in nature than the analyses presented throughout this book. Third and finally, reinterpreting how rules interact with representations can provide new insights into the nature of conspiracies. It may be the case that conspiracies are "goal oriented" but not necessarily "surface oriented". The sum of these points indicates that progress is being made in understanding the nature of conspiracies but that there still remains much to be done.

4.2   Markedness of reduplication patterns

Theoretical models that are proposed in linguistic theory should reflect in some way what is common and what is unusual in human language. These formal systems should indicate and predict what operations are more complicated than others. With the advent of linguistics becoming an active part of cognitive science in general, we must hold our formal systems to these goals. A model that does not make the correct predictions with respect to what is complex or unusual is inferior to one that makes the correct predictions.

The representational approach to reduplication proposed in this book has the characteristic that it makes predictions about the relative markedness of particular reduplication constructions. These predictions are based on the idea of analytic simplicity in that patterns that require fewer rules or less complicated rules are simpler than patterns that require multiple or more complex rules. The readjustment rules that are proposed through out chapter 3 to account for reduplicative templates have this quality. This connection between formal markedness and analytic simplicity appears to be very basic and natural but it is not reflected in other models of reduplication. No model of reduplication other than the one presented here produces these predictions or reflections of the world's languages. To show this point, let us consider the major proposals on reduplication in the past 25 years.

Carrier (1979) proposes that reduplication is best represented by a transformational rule that is present in a specific part of the morphology. The string rewrite mechanism that is the root of transformational rules does not have any inherent constraints on its application. This mechanism is able to account for all known types of reduplication but it also predicts that other unattested patterns can be produced. Thus, this mechanism overgenerates pathological reduplication patterns as easily as attested patterns. Consider the hypothetical transformations in (160).

(160) a. CVC reduplication
         CVCX   1234 → 1231234
         1 2 3 4

      b. String Reversal   1234 → 4321-1234
      c. Scrambling   1234 → 2431-1234
      d. Doubling   1234 → 11223344

All of the patterns in (160) are easily created by a transformational rule (and are equally complex, "marked", in this notation). (160a) is the analysis for prefixing CVC reduplication. The other patterns in (160b-d) are not attested in human language nor do they appear to be natural linguistic possibilities. The problem with the formal

mechanism of a transformational rule is that it is just as easy to produce the non-occurring patterns in (160b-d) as it is to produce the
occurring CVC reduplication pattern in (160a). All of the transformational patterns in (160) require four "numbers" to be used but
there is no way of predicting if the ordering of the numbers in the
output is a reasonable process or not. This situation indicates that a
transformational approach to reduplication requires additional ad
hoc mechanisms to restrict what is a possible reduplication pattern.

The next major proposal on reduplication is found in Marantz
(1982). The Marantzian approach claims that reduplication results
from the affixation of a bare CV template that triggers the copying
of the melody of the base and consequent (possibly partial) association of the copied melody to the affixed CV skeleton. Viewing
reduplication as a special kind of affixation derives constraints on
reduplication patterns from the principles of autosegmental spreading and templatic phonology that govern melody to template association.[5] In particular, the pathological patterns of reduplication
presented in (160) are difficult to produce in a Marantzian model
and are definitely predicted to be unnatural because the needed as-
sociations between melody and CV template do not follow from the
principles of autosegmental association and spreading. Other kinds
of overgeneration are possible though and more importantly, there
are no predictions made by this model about what combinations of
Cs and Vs should be possible in a reduplicative template. This
situation when combined with the approach to prespecification outlined in Marantz (1982) leads to other pathological patterns of reduplication. These new patterns are presented in (161) and we
should remember that it is not that these patterns can be produced
by the Marantzian model but that these patterns are equivalent to
occurring patterns of reduplication within this formalism.

(161) a. NoCODA effects
     badbad >> bada-badbad

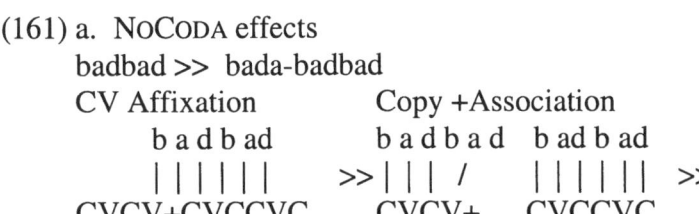

Output
b a d a b a d b a d
| | | | | | | | | |
CVCVCVCCVC

b. *radical prespecification*
badbad >> betdag-badbad

CV Affixation   Copy +Association
          b a d b ad   b a d b a d   b ad b a d
          | | | | | | >> | \ / | | | | | | >>
CVCCVC+CVCCVC   CVCCVC+   CVCCVC
  | | | | | |
  e t   g   e t   g

    Output
    b e t d a g b a d b a d
    | | | | | | | | | | | |
    CVCCVCCVC CVC

c. *radical underspecification*
badbad >> bədbəd-badbad

CV Affixation   Copy +Association
          b a d b ad   b a d b a d b ad b ad
          | | | | | | >> | / | / | | | | | | >>
CCCC+ CVCCVC   C C C C+ CVCCVC

    Epenthesis   Output
    bə d b əd b a d b a d   >>   bə d b əd b a d b a d
    | | | | | | | | | | | | | | | | | | | | | | | |
    CVCCVCCVCCVC   CVCCVCCVCCVC

The examples in (161) show that CV templates do not properly characterize naturally occurring reduplication patterns. Each example utilizes different arrangements of Cs and Vs to produce documented behavior in reduplication patterns in a pathological way.

(161a) is a case of what McCarthy and Prince (1994a) refer to as a NoCoda effect. The empirical facts of this phenomenon is that a coda consonant may not be copied as a characteristic of a reduplication pattern only if this consonant is at the end of a word or some other prosodic constituent. There are no documented cases of NoCoda effects deleting word internal codas. The particular template in (161a) only has a single intervocalic consonant so when the base melody is associated to this template there will be a word internal coda deletion in addition to the word final coda deletion which is a normal effect in some reduplication patterns. Note also that this particular pattern copies the /d/ as the onset of the second syllable in the reduplicant while the /d/ is a coda in the base. Prosodic positions do not always persist in reduplicants but NoCoda effects always preserve the prosodic identities of onsets/codas in the reduplicant. This result indicates that the Marantzian model of reduplication is like the Optimality Theory model in that both models predict that a pathological NoCoda reduplication pattern that deletes word internal codas is as likely as naturally occurring reduplication patterns.

Example (161b), referred to as *radical prespecification*, shows that if some melodies are allowed to be preassociated to a reduplicative template then unnatural reduplication patterns can be easily produced. Marantz (1982:449-450) utilizes this approach to account for some aspects of reduplication in Akan and Yoruba so this example is predicted to be a possible reduplication pattern. Prespecification in reduplication patterns is limited to a single prespecified region so the discontinuous prespecification in (161b) does not appear to be a natural phenomenon. As with (161a), this type of prespecification is as likely as other naturally occurring types of prespecification according to the Marantzian model of reduplication and this is a liability.

(161c) is referred to as *radical underspecification* because this example posits a template that consists solely of C slots. This allows the consonantal melody from the base to associate to the template with the result of producing a string of consonants. This string of four consonants will violate the syllable structure of most languages and epenthesis will then insert vowels (default vowels by assumption, for this example /ə/) in order to remedy the consonant clusters. The end effect of this type of template is the surface appearance of all the vowels in the base being overwritten by default vowels in the reduplicant. This effect may also relocate the vowels in the reduplicant depending on the particular epenthesis rules of a given language. An analogous default consonant effect can be produced in a language that does not allow onsetless syllables by affixing a template full of V slots. Consonants would then be inserted to create onsets for the vowel initial syllables producing the effect that consonants (and possibly consonant clusters) are overwritten by default onsets. As with the two previous examples, CV templates do not distinguish between this example of pathological reduplication and naturally occurring reduplication patterns.

As with the transformational model of reduplication, the Marantz (1982) CV affix model of reduplication requires additional ad hoc constraints to limit the types of CV templates that can be affixed. This indicates that this mechanism misses a generalization about reduplicative templates.

A proposal that builds on Marantz's work is Prosodic Morphology (McCarthy and Prince 1986). The relevant claim here made by Prosodic Morphology is that templates are not composed of C and V slots but instead they consist of prosodic structures. McCarthy and Prince's proposal limits all templates to authentic units of prosody which are Wd "prosodic word", F "foot", σ "syllable", σ_μ "light (monomoraic) syllable", $\sigma_{\mu\mu}$ "heavy (bimoraic) syllable" and finally σ_c "core syllable" (McCarthy and Prince 1986:6).

Restricting templates to only legitimate prosodic categories only removes the type of overgeneration seen in (161c). The pathological reduplication patterns in (161a,b) are still produced using prosodic categories because the effects describe prosodic categories. NOCODA effects result from using light syllables (σ_μ) in the reduplicative template. A trochaic foot can consist of two light syllables, thus (161a) can still be produced by specifying the template as [$\sigma_\mu\sigma_\mu$]. In fact, if the position that core syllables (σ_c) are less marked than other syllables, then the mechanisms in Prosodic Morphology actually predict that medial coda omission in reduplication is less marked than other patterns because a LL trochaic foot would be relatively unmarked. Changing to using prosodic units to define templates does not affect the preassociation of elements so the pathological prespecification seen in (161b) is also a reasonable reduplication pattern within Prosodic Morphology. In other words, the revision of the Marantz (1982) model of reduplication through the adoption of Prosodic Morphology does little to change the predictions made about what is a natural or unnatural in a reduplication pattern.

The final derivational model of reduplication that needs to be discussed is the full copy model proposed by Steriade (1988). Steriade claims that reduplication copies the entire melodic and prosodic structure of a form and then deletes parts of this structure in the reduplicant according to the setting of certain parameters. These parameters, according to Steriade, encode markedness effects by indicating what prosodic structures should be eliminated or simplified in the reduplicant.

This approach has the advantage that total reduplication is easily accounted for and its commonness is predicted by the nature the proposal. Since full reduplication is accomplished by simply copying the whole structure and doing nothing else, it is predicted to be the default case of reduplication. This fact is supported by the prevalence of total reduplication in the world's languages and this generalization should be embedded in any adequate model of reduplication. The parameters posited by Steriade only eliminate marked prosodic structure in that they limit what structures are licensed. Thus, one parameter can be set to "core syllable" and this will eliminate all branching structure in a syllable in the reduplicant. Other parameters will simplify complex onsets, remove codas, specify the prosodic weight of the reduplicant, etc.

The parameters proposed by Steriade and their effects do not make the correct generalizations about reduplication patterns though. The full copy model predicts that unattested reduplication patterns should be more common than some attested ones. The reason behind this is due to how total reduplication is handled in this model. Total reduplication is predicted to be the most common pattern because no parameters are active in this pattern. Only the full copy process is required. This is a correct generalization.

Following this point, patterns of reduplication that require fewer parameter settings should be more common than patterns requiring a greater number of parameter settings. This prediction is problematic for the following reason. CV reduplication results from the interaction of three parameters: the weight parameter, the complex onset parameter, and the coda parameter. The troublesome prediction that is present here is that a reduplication pattern that results from the omission of one of these parameters should be less marked than CV reduplication. Omitting either of the two syllable parameters (complex onset and coda) is not problematic but omission of the weight parameter is. The weight parameter reduces the reduplicant to a single mora and monomoraic reduplication patterns in the world's languages do show simplification of onsets and limitations on possible codas. It is only when there is no weight parameter that the other two parameters become problematic. Consider the example in (162).

(162) *Parameter*: complex onset
   Setting: unmarked (=complex onsets not allowed)
   Matching procedure: Eliminate from the base a unit disallowed by the template.

   Parameter: obstruent codas
   Setting: unmarked (=obstruent codas disallowed)
   Matching procedure: Eliminate from the base a unit disallowed by the template.

Base:	bradbrad
Full Copy:	bradbrad-bradbrad
Complex Onset:	badbad-bradbrad
Obstruent Coda:	baba-bradbrad

The derivation in (162) produces the pathological NoCoda reduplication pattern. Additionally, word internal onsets are simplified which also does not appear to occur in natural human languages. These results show that there must be additional ad hoc constraints placed on the relationship between certain parameters. The pathological reduplication pattern in (162) is predicted to occur by the full copy model because it utilizes only two parameters while CV reduplication results from three parameters. An additional problem to the full copy approach is that to produce unmarked prosodic patterns in the reduplicant, formally marked structures in the form of additional parameters are posited. This situation is contradictory in nature and indicates that the formal system underlying the full copy model of reduplication is inherently flawed.

Optimality Theory has made no advances on the problem of overgenerating reduplicative templates over previous models of reduplication. Stemberger (1996) shows that all problems of overgeneration that plague prior models of reduplication also affect present Optimality Theory proposals. Producing the pathological NOCODA effect Optimality Theory has already been discussed in chapter 3 and (163) presents this crucial tableau that shows how this effect is produced again.

(163)

RED+tagtagtag	NO CODA	MAX$_{BR}$	CONTIGUITY
a. tagtagtag-tagtagtag	****!**		
b. tagtagta-tagtagtag	****!*	*	
☞ c. tatata-tagtagtag	***	***	**

Candidate (163c) is the most harmonic given the constraint ranking in (163) because it has eliminated all codas in the reduplicant. Since MAX$_{BR}$ and CONTIGUITY are both ranked below NOCODA, the elimination of all codas in the reduplicant is the expected behavior.

Stemberger also shows that string reversal patterns can also be produced in Optimality Theory. Consider the tableau in (164) from Stemberger (1996).

(164)

/akison/	ONSET	CONTIGUITY	LINEARITY	ANCHORING
a. akison	*!			
☞ b. nosika			*...	*...
c. kasino		*!	*...	*...
d. nakiso		*!	*...	*...

Stemberger argues that if epenthesis and deletion are ruled out as possible repairs to ONSET violations (by ranking FAITH$_{BR}$ above MAX and DEP), then string reversal as seen in candidate (164b) is a possible response within Optimality Theory grammars. This does not appear to occur in natural languages. This result indicates that Optimality Theory is roughly equivalent in power to the transformational model of Carrier (1979) with respect to templates. This is a move backwards in the understanding of reduplication patterns because Marantzian models of reduplication blocked string reversal patterns. This is one concrete ill effect of the addition of parallel computation and transderivational information to phonology.

A pattern similar to the radical underspecification effect illustrated in the Marantzian model of reduplication in (161c) can also be easily produced by Optimality Theory. This pattern is produced by ranking MAX$_{BR}$ below featural markedness constraints which causes only default segments to occur in the reduplicant. This is phonological fixed segmentism according to Alderete et al (1999). Consider the hypothetical example of this in (165).

(165)

RED+tagtagtag	V-MARKEDNESS	V-MAX$_{BR}$
a. tagtagtag-tagtagtag	****!**	
b. təgtagtag-tagtagtag	****!*	*
c. təgtəgtag-tagtagtag	****!	**
☞ d. təgtəgtəg-tagtagtag	***	***

Candidate (165d) is the most harmonic given the constraint ranking in (165) since it has reduced all of the vowels in the reduplicant to an unmarked vowel (/ə/ for this particular example). This type of prespecification does not appear to occur in natural human languages. Prespecification only appears to occur in a single region or span in a reduplication construction. Optimality Theory approaches to reduplication do not capture this generalization.

Optimality Theory also introduces a new type of pathological reduplication pattern unproducable in other models of reduplication. Due to the possibility of backcopying effects, Optimality Theory can produce the backcopying of a templatic requirement in reduplicated forms. McCarthy and Prince (1997) refer to this problem as the Kager-Hamilton problem.

The root of the Kager-Hamilton problem is that correspondence theory accounts for and predicts backcopying effects should exist in reduplication. This is the correct result for segmental processes but there are no attested cases of the backcopying of prosodic structure. A tableau showing the hypothetical backcopying of a reduplicative template that is the root of the Kager-Hamilton problem is presented in (166) (McCarthy and Prince 1997:30).

(166)

	/RED+tilparku/	RED=MinWd	MAX$_{BR}$	MAX$_{IO}$
☞	a. tilpa-tilpa			*
	b. tilpa-tilparku		*!	
	c. tilparku-tilparku	*!		

The tableau in (166) shows that if a templatic constraint and MAX$_{BR}$ are ranked above MAX$_{IO}$, a backcopying effect based on the template which truncates the base can be produced. This type of effect is unknown in human language.

The immediate response to this dilemma by McCarthy and Prince is to eliminate "templates" from Optimality Theory. This move does not affect Optimality Theory's ability to produce the Hamilton-Kager problem though. If we replace RED=MinWd with a generalized alignment constraint that requires RED to right-align with a heavy syllable (as was done for the Ilokano example in section 4.1) a truncation effect is still produced. Consider the tableau in (167).

(167)

	/RED+tilparku/	ALIGN(RED, σ$_{\mu\mu}$)	MAX$_{BR}$	MAX$_{IO}$
	a. tilparku-tilparku	*!		*
☞	b. tilpar-tilpar			**
	c. tilpar-tilparku		*!*	
	d. til-til			***!**

Candidate (167a) shows total reduplication and the reduplicant is not right-aligned with a heavy syllable. The winning candidate in

(167b) has a reduplicant that is right-aligned with a heavy syllable and truncation of the base to satisfy MAX$_{BR}$. Candidate (167c) shows a correctly aligned reduplicant but no truncation in the base and this candidate fares worse than the winning one on MAX-BR. Finally candidate (167d) presents a candidate that gratuitously truncates and is consequently less harmonic.

The required response to remove the Hamilton-Kager problem from Optimality Theory is the placement of ad hoc meta-constraints that limit what constraint rankings can occur. Spaelti (1997) proposes that base/reduplicant faithfulness can not be ranked higher than input/output faithfulness and that this would block pathological backcopying of templates from occurring in Optimality Theory. This solution only indicates that the basic mechanism of constraint ranking does not make the correct typological predictions of what reduplication patterns should or should not occur. The fact that Optimality Theory requires additional ad hoc restrictions indicates that it is missing a basic generalization about reduplication.

We now see that overgeneration plagues all proposals on reduplication (Stemberger 1996) to a greater or lesser extent. Overgeneration itself can be overcome through a theory of simplicity and learning (Chomsky 1975, Chomsky and Halle 1968) but whether or not a model makes predictions about the behavior of reduplication is an inherent aspect of the particular model. None of the previous models of reduplication make the correct predictions about markedness of reduplication patterns.

The model of reduplication proposed in this book does make correct predictions about what reduplication patterns are more marked than others based on the idea of analytic simplicity. Total reduplication is the formally unmarked pattern of reduplication according to these proposals since only reference to the beginning and end of a precedence graph is required. These two positions only require reference to # and %. All other reduplication patterns must make reference to other points in a precedence graph and these points are more formally marked because of their more complicated environments. Prefixing CV reduplication makes reference to the "first vowel" which is a more complicated environment because segmental features (or possibly syllable structure) must be included in this calculation. Prefixing CVC reduplication makes reference to an element that follows the first vowel and is consequently more analytically marked than CV reduplication. As the different patterns of reduplication were discussed and analyzed in section 3.4, the precedence variables utilized in these analyses became more and more complicated. This situation makes the prediction that as the precedence variables become more complicated the resulting reduplication pattern is more marked.

As shown in chapter 3, the present proposals on reduplication are unable to create the pathological NOCODA effect in a productive fashion. Consider the precedence structure in (168) which presents what a pathological NOCODA precedence graph would look like.

(168)
$$\# \to t \to a \to g \to t \to a \to g \to t \to a \to g \to \%$$

The discussion of this precedence graph in chapter 3 indicates that since an additional jump link must be added for each coda in the base and since the number of codas in the base is variable there is no way to provide a generalization as to how many coda deleting jump links must be added as part of this reduplication pattern. This type of argument has been previously used by Carrier (1979) and McCarthy and Prince (1986) to argue that CV templates are incapable of providing a generalization for total reduplication.

The variable number of links needed to produce a certain surface effect also prevents the model of reduplication proposed here from productively creating patterns of string reversal, radical underspecification, and radical prespecification. Consider the precedence graphs in (169). Each graph presents one of the pathological types of reduplication patterns produced in previous models of reduplication.

(169) a. *string reversal*

$$\# \to t \to a \to g \to t \to a \to g \to \%$$

b. *radical prespecification*

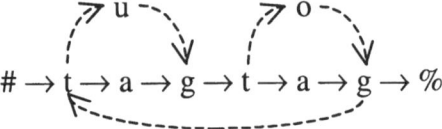

c. *radical underspecification*

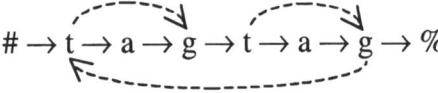

Each graph in (169) has the characteristic that the number of precedence links that are required to produce the surface effect is dependent on some aspect of the base. The string reversal pattern in (169a) requires the addition of X+1 links where X is the number of segments in the base. The radical prespecification example in (169b) requires a separate "morpheme" which specifies what prespecified segment should appear for each separate prespecified region. As with the other examples, the number of required prespecified regions is dependent on the content of the base. Finally, (169c) presents a case of radical underspecification where jump links are added over every vowel in the base. Presumably, after linearization an epenthesis process will then break up the resulting consonant clusters. As with the other pathological patterns of reduplication, the radical underspecification pattern requires a number of precedence links to be added to the base where the number of links is dependent on some aspect of the base.

The types of pathological reduplication patterns that are obtainable in previous models of reduplication can not be productively characterized in the present model. All of these pathological reduplication patterns share the characteristic that part of the pattern is directly dependent on some variable aspect of the base (number of segments, number of vowels, number of consonants, etc.). Due to this variable aspect, the present model of reduplication can not produce these patterns in a generative way. This is a welcomed result.

That analytic simplicity derives the formal markedness of reduplication patterns in the system developed here and that this system of markedness reflects typological facts about human language sets the model of reduplication developed in this book apart from all other models. No other theory of reduplication has this characteristic. All other models make incorrect predictions about what reduplication patterns should be more marked than others. This fact strongly indicates that the model of reduplication proposed here provides a deeper insight into human language than any other model of reduplication.

4.3   Reduplication specific mechanisms

A final argument to support the superiority of the approach to reduplication proposed in this book is based on reduplication specific machinery and how this issue relates to the presence of reduplication in natural human languages.

All previous theories of reduplication have what could be considered "core phonology" and then there is some sort of special mechanism or account of reduplication. For Carrier (1979), the special status of reduplication is reflected in the utilization of transformational rules. For Marantz (1982) and other affix and copy approaches, reduplication is the result of a special affix that triggers a special copy process. The additional copying of melody from the base which is crucial to the Marantz model of reduplication is stipulated and not derived from any principle. Optimality Theory approaches to reduplication retain the special affixation aspect of the Marantzian approach through the adoption of RED as an abstract morpheme which conditions its own cophonology, base/reduplicant correspondence.

An aspect common to all of these previous approaches to reduplication is that reduplication could be eliminated from these theories of phonology if the special mechanism or affix is eliminated. Generative phonology at the time of Carrier (1979) could operate perfectly well without transformational rules. The same can be said of phonological theory at the time of Marantz (1982). Phonological theory at these times provided analyses for non-reduplicated phenomena without using any aspects of the technology introduced to account for reduplication. Optimality Theory is the same way in that if reduplication did not exist, Optimality Theory would be just as viable a theory of grammar without RED and base/reduplicant correspondence. This situation makes the prediction that reduplication is not a core characteristic of human language in these models of phonology. The logical result of this finding is that there should be some languages that do not have reduplication of any kind. This prediction is not supported though, Moravcsik (1978) indicates that total reduplication may be a true universal feature of natural human language.

The model of reduplication developed here does not have any reduplication specific machinery. All technology utilized in accounting for reduplication is necessary for any aspect of phonology to operate in this model. Precedence relations are required in phonological representations because of distinctive phonological representations that do not differ in segmental content. Representations like /tæk/ and /kæt/ only differ in the precedence relationships in the representations. They are identical if only segmental content is considered.

If we remove reduplication from our thoughts for a moment and consider the way precedence is represented in the model proposed here, one of the most natural questions that one would ask is what happens if more than a single arrow (precedence relation) connects to a segment. The reintroduction of explicit precedence relations in phonological representations immediately begs the question of what predictions do more complex precedence structures make. Chapters 2 and 3 of this book provide the initial answers to this question. New insights into reduplication and infixation are immediately gained by asking what more complicated precedence structures would be like. To rule out these more complicated precedence structures once we have explicit precedence we would actually have to stipulate the conditions of asymmetry and irreflexiveness on precedence structures. A system that lacks these requirements is logically simpler and consequently arguments must be provided to adopt the more logically complex and restricted model of precedence. The analysis of reduplication presented throughout this book indicates that arguing for required asymmetry and irreflexiveness in phonological representations would only eliminate the empirical and theoretical successes documented in this book. No benefits would be gained.

The linearization process is a bare output condition (Chomsky 1995) that is imposed because phonological representations must be interpretable by the phonetics module. Since the phonetics module must eventually produce representations that are motor control programs, phonetic representations are more restricted in nature. Linearization is a requirement that any model of phonology must incorporate in some way. If phonological representations are not linearized then they will be uninterpretable at the phonetics-phonology interface. The one interesting aspect of the view of linearization presented in this book is that it operates within the phonology and not just at the end of the phonological component. This is a surprising finding that could not be discovered by other approaches that did not consider the more complex precedence structures investigated here. This finding also provides more evidence for the importance of intermediate representations in phonology.

The final component of the analysis of reduplication that was added to phonological theory is the Uniformity Parameter. In essence this parameter is equivalent to other common parameters found on phonological rules such as Structure Preservation or the Derived Environment Condition (Kiparsky 1982). All parameters like these are present in all phonological rules although they may not be active or may even be irrelevant given the structure of a given phonological rule. This does not make any of these parameters specific to a particular construction, they are part of the theory of phonological rules. There is a general schema provided by universal grammar for a phonological rule and the analyses presented in this book have only identified another feature of this schema. This discovery is totally dependent on the consideration of more complex precedence structures and this explains why this aspect of phonological rules has not be discovered previously.

Because no part of the analysis of reduplication can be eliminated from the model of phonology used in this book without impacting the entire system, we can conclude that reduplication is derived from general principles in this model of phonology. Since reduplication follows from other independently needed mechanisms, this model of reduplication makes the surprising prediction that reduplication should occur in all human languages. Combining the complete integration of reduplication within phonology with the functional view that total reduplication results in a very large surface difference through the minimal addition of phonological material (only a single bare precedence relation) the cross-linguistic commonness of reduplication is not a surprise at all. No other model of reduplication provides this insight into reduplication. Consequently, this argues strongly for the precedence based model of reduplication developed here.

4.4 Conclusion

A new representational theory of reduplication based on the clarification of precedence relations and structures in morphophonological representations has been presented. This approach has made discoveries about the nature of phonology, morphology, and the interaction between morphology and phonology. The combination of the views of grammar proposed in chapters 2 and 3 provide a guide to the issues in phonology and morphology that can be illuminated further by the proposals in this book.

One of the most important issues that must be investigated further is the nature of the timing tier in phonological representations. The core of this question is how precedence information is percolated into feature geometries. The strong position on this issue is to limit primitive precedence information to the timing tier and have all other precedence relations between autosegmental features be derived from the timing tier. This view makes the claim that precedence is only relevant at the timing tier and all other tiers are unordered and only receive precedence relationships through their connection to the timing tier. An alternative to this view is to have each autosegmental tier contain precedence information and then provide some way of synchronizing the precedence information across the independent tiers. Whatever view of precedence turns out to be correct, the locality of phonological processes is affected by the way precedence is encoded so there will likely be discoveries about locality in phonology that result from the further study of precedence.

Many other phonological issues are directly impacted by the proposals made here. The most obvious one is hopefully a renewed interest in serial models of phonology. This approach to phonology has fallen by the wayside without much discussion. Serial based models have advantages to them that are not being used in current research and this is unfortunate. One of the main advantages is the reduction of the interaction between phonological rules and reduplication to being an opacity effect. Considering this result, it is not entirely clear that there is any evidence for parallel computation or transderivational rules in phonology since backcopying reduplication effects are the main argument in favor of these views. It is interesting to note that the effect that is required to account for these backcopying effects is for a single phonological entity to be "in two places at once". McCarthy and Prince (1995) interpret this situation to require parallel computation but we see a simpler possibility in chapter 2 to account for this behavior. Looping structures in phonological representations create this exact "two places at once" situation but yet still retain Markovian computation. If parallel computation is present in phonology, we have to look at places other than reduplication to find the evidence for it.

Moving beyond the general issue of computation in phonology, two more specific issues may receive additional insight from the proposals here. The first one is geminate integrity (Schein and Steriade 1986). The question of whether geminates are best represented in the traditional autosegmental way of two timing units and only a single melodic unit or represented by a single timing unit that loops back onto itself is presently an open one. In chapter 2 and 3 we have found cases of both types of geminates. In fact Tohono O'odham appears to be a language that uses both types of representations for long vowels as indicated by the analysis in chapter 3 (pp. 115-116). Regardless of whether there are multiple possibilities for the representation of geminates or there is only a single possible representation, geminate integrity effects should result from the setting of the Uniformity Parameter on a given rule. Since geminates share with reduplication the "two places at once" characteristic both situations should behave in similar ways. Following from this, geminate inalterability is equivalent to underapplication in reduplication and lack of geminate inalterability is overapplication. Whichever of these behaviors result will be predicted by the setting of the Uniformity Parameter of a given rule. An immediate question for this approach is whether post-linearization rules respect geminate integrity effects. If this is the case, then it appears that both classical geminate structures and reflexive self-loops are not affected by linearization. If there are no post-linearization geminate inalterability effects then this indicates that geminates are linearized in a way that ensures an irreflexive and asymmetrical representation is produced. The decision between these two options is presently an open empirical question and this question can only be asked due to the advances made in the understanding of precedence in phonology by the present proposals.

The other topic that may become better understood through the present proposals is metathesis. The phenomenon of metathesis, where two segments change their precedence relationships, is a puzzle in a model of phonology that does not recognize explicit precedence relationships. The model proposed here provides a framework that can directly describe what the process of metathesis is doing. The questions that must be addressed is whether metathesis is productive or lexicalized in particular languages, what are the conditioning environments (functional or formal), and what are the limits on the application of this process (why does metathesis appear to be only a local operation). Answers to these questions will further our understanding of how precedence is manipulated in phonological representations.

In relation to morphology, two topics are immediately relevant to the proposals made here. The first one is to investigate the nature of truncation morphology (Benua 1995). Formally, the system proposed in this thesis makes the prediction that truncation should be one of the most productive morphological changes found in human language because it will be relatively unmarked. Interestingly, surface truncation effects will be produced in the present model through the addition of phonological material. Specifically, a precedence link will be added from somewhere in a word to the end symbol or from the beginning symbol to somewhere in word. Both situations effectively add a "detour" possibility that will be used by the linearization process. This detour is similar to infixation as seen in the analysis of Sundanese in chapter 3 and the multiple environments created by this kind of detour provide an immediate explanation for the over- and underapplication effects in truncation identified by Benua (1995). We should be cautious about how we proceed with analyses of truncation because most cases of truncation morphology that are discussed in the literature do not appear to be fully productive. It is entirely possible to produce lexical analyses of most truncation patterns that are just as viable as productive ones.[6] Only further work on this type of phenomenon will allow us to determine what the best way is to precede and the model of precedence proposed here provides a natural way to form interesting questions about this topic.

The other major morphological issue that is directly related to the proposals in chapter 3 is the analysis of non-concatenative morphology. Hints of a new view of this type of morphological system can be seen in the analysis of Chaha in chapter 2 and infixes in chapter 3. It may be possible to revive a purely concatenative account of Semitic morphology based on a Prince (1977) view of underlying forms in Semitic in conjunction with the proposals made here in relation to infixes. Ussishkin (1999) appears to be moving in this general direction with the claim that the notion of root is inadequate to account for some phenomenon in Modern Hebrew. In response to this Ussishkin develops a melodic overwriting analysis and considering the discussion of this topic in chapter 3 we can see how this proposal provides a new approach to understanding root and template morphological systems. This approach would have the benefit of reducing concatenative and non-concatenative models of morphology to the same type of system with the difference residing in the type of precedence variables used. This would be a major advance in our understanding of morphological systems and human language in general.

A final note on the relationship between morphology and reduplication is that it should be obvious from this work that morphological analysis is crucial to understand the behavior of reduplication. Recent work by Inkelas and Zoll (1999, 2000ab, Inkelas 2000, Zoll 2000) also calls attention to this point. The points made by Inkelas and Zoll are fully compatible with the proposals made in this book because of the assumption of modularity between morphology and phonology. Since the explanation for the behavior of reduplicated forms is distributed between these two modules in the model developed here, the morphological phenomena that Inkelas and Zoll focus on can be explained within the morphology and the phonological phenomena focused on by McCarthy and Prince (1995) can be explained in the phonology. Inkelas and Zoll (2000b) spend a great deal of time indicating where the McCarthy and Prince (1995) model of reduplication is incapable of accounting for some morphological aspects of phonology but they fail to show that their morphological doubling theory is capable of accounting for the full range of backcopying effects. Certain cases of backcopying effects are reanalyzed by Inkelas and Zoll as simple over- or underapplication effects by altering the ordering of morphemes in these cases. Inkelas and Zoll (1999, 2000ab, Inkelas 2000, Zoll 2000) have failed to address cases of backcopying where the ordering of morphemes can not be manipulated. Two such cases of backcopying have been analyzed here and they are the case of nasal spread in Malay and Chaha /x/ dissimilation both in chapter 2. An additional case of backcopying of this flavor appears in Abkhaz (Bruening 1997) where placement of an epenthetic vowel in reduplicated forms is backcopied into the stem. Nothing has been said about these types of backcopying by Inkelas and Zoll. Until these recalcitrant cases of backcopying are accounted for within morphological doubling theory (Inkelas and Zoll 2000b)[7], the only lesson we learn from Inkelas and Zoll is that we must pay attention to the morphological aspects of reduplication.

In final summary, this book presents a novel way of looking at precedence in phonological representations. The immediate benefits of this new view can be seen in respect to reduplication. Hopefully, the results presented in this book will lead to future research that provides deeper insight into our understanding of human language.

Notes

Chapter 2

1. Transitivity is not true of the precedence relation if immediate precedence is used instead.
2. The issue of how geminates are represented presents an interesting question to this claim. At the melodic level, geminates are only a single entity while at the timing level or X tier, they are two segments. This arrangement may allow a position that a geminate precedes itself but only if you allow reference across both the X and melodic tiers. It is the reference across two tiers of representations that makes geminates appear to be non-irreflexive segments and there are no cases of non-irreflexivity if the domain of relation is limited to a single level.
3. Non-asymmetrical and symmetrical are not the same. Non-asymmetrical indicates that a particular relation is neither asymmetrical nor symmetrical. This situation also holds for non-irreflexive.
4. Irreflexivity may not be a required characteristic of phonological representations depending on how geminates are represented. A geminate segment can be represented with a precedence link that loops back to the originating segment. The question here is whether a segment that has a loop back onto itself can be interpreted as representing a long segment. If this is interpretable by the phonetics module, then irreflexivity is not removed during the linearization process. Geminates and other long segments are not a prime concern of the present work so the full ramifications of the present proposals for the representation of length will be left for future research.
5. Marantz (1982:461 fn.) takes issue with this claim. Marantz points out that the evidence for the palatalization rule is sketchy because there are velars that occur in environments where palatalization should have occurred. The fact that Wilbur (1973) claims that palatalization is a rule of Akan is explained by Marantz as an effort to reduce the amount of underlying phonemes in the inventory of Akan. McCarthy and Prince (1995:341 fn.) state that all analyses of Akan need to account for the palatalization facts. I will remain noncommittal on this issue but will follow McCarthy and Prince (1995) in presenting a palatalization based analysis of Akan in order to facilitate comparison between the proposals in this book and McCarthy and Prince (1995).
6. /a/ is specified as [-back] and thus /ɪ/ occurs in words that have /a/ in them. /u/ results in reduplicated forms that have a [back] vowel in the root, i.e. *su-so* 'seize' McCarthy and Prince (1995:331), Schachter and Fromkin (1968).
7. The [coronal] feature of these two vowels is actually shared as indicated below in (i).

i.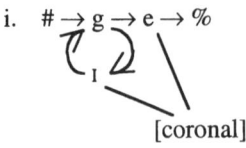

       [coronal]

8. The alternation between /r/~/n/ seen in this form is due to a general nasalization process of medial sonorants; see Banksira (1997:108-109)
9. /K/ surfaces as [a] (Banksira 1997, Kenstowicz and Banksira 1999).
10. See Ussishkin (1999) for proposals characterizing root and template type nonconcatenative morphology as melodic overwriting.
11. Kenstowicz and Banksira (1999) discuss how this process could be generalized to be the result of a broader OCP effect on all continuants. The sketch of this approach is based on gaps in the continuant series of phonemes in Chaha. Kenstowicz and Banksira correctly point out that this issue is orthogonal to the discussion of backcopying in Chaha. I follow them in leaving aside a stronger and more formal discussion of exactly what the root of the /x/ dissimilation process is.
12. /β/ is [+sonorant] according to Kenstowicz and Banksira (1999: fn. 1) and thus does not trigger the [x] ... [-sonorant, +cont] constraint.
13. This vowel sometimes appears as /ə/, *tə-rxa̰xəβ* frequentive imperative of /rxβ/ 'show up' (Kenstowicz and Banksira 1999:581).
14. I would like to thank Sharon Rose for explicating this aspect of Chaha morphology for me. I take full responsibility for any mistakes present in this work on this topic.

Chapter 3

1. See Anderson (1992) for extensive arguments against morphological information within the phonological component.
2. Homophony of affixes can complicate this point. With respect to reduplication, a homophony alternative would posit the same reduplication pattern as the exponent of different morpho-syntactic features. The readjustment approach to reduplication advocated here reduces the amount of homophony in the morphological component by allowing different morpho-syntactic features to trigger a single rule.
3. Morphemes themselves will only add phonological material but there is the possibility that a given morpheme may trigger a readjustment rule that deletes a feature. This type of process is referred to as impoverishment (Bonet 1991, Noyer 1997) and see Noyer (1998) for a discussion of the implications of this type of operation.
4. Raimy (1999) implements this updating process through the use of *stacks* as the data structure that encodes precedence. The nature of a stack makes the most recently added material the most accessible since it is at the "top" of the

stack. If the concatenation of morphemes is the addition of information to a stack, then what segment is at the beginning or end of a precedence structure is calculated by what is at the top of the # stack and what stack has % at its top respectively. See Raimy (1999) for the full details of this implementation of precedence in phonological representations.

5. There is one exception to this generalization, *búri-al*.

6. The transparency of /h/ and /ʔ/ in the nasal spread process is due to them not being "supraglottally articulated consonant[s]" (Robins 1957:90) thus not having a [place] feature and consequently being [-cons].

7. In the model of phonology described here, there is the uninteresting possibility of prespecification imposed by the phonology when some sort of neutralization rule prevents a contrast from appearing in certain instances. Aspects of the analysis of Nancowry developed in this section will have this characteristic but this is phonological prespecification in only a trivial and uninteresting sense and will not be discussed further.

8. An additional condition on the coda in the reduplicant is that palatal stops, /c/, copy as coronals, /t/. In the approach that will be developed here, this change in coda can be considered the result of the deletion of the palatal feature on the coronal node due to a coda licensing restriction in unstressed syllables.

9. To be precise, the only codas present in unstressed non-reduplicated syllables are /n/ and /m/. Reduplicated syllables add the oral stops and /ŋ/ to the inventory of codas in unstressed syllables.

10. The /a/ is a suffix marking "objective" (Radhakrishnan 1981:66) and is not part of the root.

11. A plausible alternative formulation of the reduplication pattern in Nancowry is to specify an affix of # → {i,u} → "last segment" which triggers a readjustment rule of total reduplication.

12. This is only a sample of the complete data set that Uhrbach (1987) presents. Forms that show the behavior of the unspecified nasal segment in relation to sonorants and /h/ are omitted because these sequences do not show overapplication effects.

13. There is the other possibility that the coalescence rule requires the segments that are going to be coalesced to share a place feature. This too would restrict the application of this process to only affixes that contain an underspecified nasal segment.

14. There is the interesting possibility that the two different representations for "long" affect other aspects of grammar. One possibility that should be investigated further is that whether long vowels count as heavy in the metrical component is dependent on how length is represented. Self-loop long vowels could be always interpreted as light since there is only a single timing unit that is repeated while the traditional geminate structure representation could indicate that a long vowel should be interpreted as heavy due to its two distinct timing units. How the metrical grid projects from the novel precedence structures proposed here is an important area that must be left to future research.

15. This section has benefited greatly from questions raised by Bruce Hayes at the *Phonology 2000* conference at MIT and Harvard in the spring of 1999.
16. Note that this claim of bi-directional copying violates arguments by Urbanczyk (1996) that the base for a reduplicant consists of the string of segments that occurs to the left or right of the reduplicant. In other words, the implications of Urbanczyk's analysis of reduplication in Lushootseed predict that the analysis proposed by Jones for Mangarrayi is impossible.
17. Two aspects that must be noted for this reduplication pattern in Temiar are the following. The macron over a vowel indicates tenseness and not length (Benjamin 1976). The reduplicated form of *rec* has a /ɲ/ in the reduplicant instead of /c/. This is due to a process that either voices or nasalizes codas (Benjamin 1976:143).

Chapter 4

1. Not only is this approach to reduplicative templates contradictory to the generalized template theory approach but it will also allows pathological reduplication patterns to emerge. McCarthy and Prince (1997) discus the "Hamilton-Kager" problem where the existence of "templates" predicts that templatic requirements on RED could backcopy onto the stem leading to truncation of the base. This does not occur in natural human languages therefore McCarthy and Prince move to eliminate "templates" from phonological theory. This is one of the main motivations for generalized template theory. See section 4.2 for further discussion.
2. This is under the assumption that base and stem are coextensive. This is not a necessary assumption in Optimality Theory analyses of reduplication and there does not appear to be any consensus as to how the base is calculated in reduplication. See Idsardi and Raimy (to appear) for a discussion of this issue and the computational/learnability problems that it raises for Optimality Theory.
3. This assumes that the range of input-output calculation in reduplication structures covers the entire output structure and not just the base as in proposals by Raimy and Idsardi (1997) and Struijke (1998).
4. For a similar discussion of a possible conspiracy argument based on coda neutralization in Korean see Idsardi and Kim (forthcoming).
5. The issue of exactly how melody/template association proceeded was a very active issue in the literature following Marantz (1982). Marantz proposed and argued for a template driven type of association where the template was primary in the association process. Others proposed different positions on this topic though. Kitagawa (1987), Mester (1988), Clements (1985), and Cowper and Rice (1985) among others all present different views on this topic. See these authors for arguments for their particular positions.

6. Utilizing present proposals, a "lexical" analysis of a truncation pattern would posit an underlying precedence structure that contained the jump link that would demarcate the truncated form. Once given this representation, we would only have to provide a way to indicate whether to use the "short" path through the precedence structure (producing the truncated form) or to use the "long" path through the precedence structure (producing the non-truncated form).

7. Even if backcopying effects are given an explanation within morphological doubling theory (Inkelas and Zoll 2000b), the arguments against Optimality Theory in general based on markedness of reduplication patterns discussed in section 4.2 still hold. Consequently, morphological doubling theory has both empirical and conceptual issues that must be addressed.

References

Alderete, John, Jill Beckman, Laura Benua, Amalia Gnanadesikan, John McCarthy and Suzanne Urbanczyk
    1999   Reduplication with fixed segmentism. *Linguistic Inquiry* 30.3: 327-364.

Anderson, Stephen
    1980   *The organization of phonology*. New York: Academic Press.
    1992   *A-morphous morphology*. Cambridge: Cambridge University Press.

Applegate, Richard
    1976   Reduplication in Chumash. In: Margaret Langdon and Shirley Silver (eds.) *Hokan studies,* 271-283. The Hague: Mouton.

Archangeli, Diana and D. Terrence Langedoen
    1997   *Optimality Theory: An Overview*. New York: Blackwells.

Archangeli, Diana and Douglas Pulleyblank
    1994   *Grounded phonology*. Cambridge, Mass.: MIT Press.

Avery, Peter and William Idsardi
    to appear Laryngeal dimensions, completion and enhancement. In: *Proceedings from the conference on distinctive features*. Zentrum für Allegeine Sprachwissenschaft, Berlin, Oct. 1999.

Bagemihl, Bruce
    1989   Syllable structure in Bella Coola. *Linguistic Inquiry*, 22: 589-646.

Banksira, Degif Petros
    1997   The sound system of Chaha. Ph.D. dissertation, Université du Québec á Montréal.

Beckman, Jill
    1995   Shona height harmony: Markedness and positional identity. In: *University of Massachusetts occasional papers in linguistics 18: Papers in Optimality Theory*, 53-76. GLSA, University of Massachusetts, Amherst.

Benjamin, Geoffrey
    1976   An Outline of Temiar Grammar. In: Philip N. Jenner, Laurence C. Thompson and Stanley Starosta (eds.) *Austroasiatic Studies*, Part I. 129-187.

Benua, Laura
    1995   Identity effects in morphological truncation. In: *University of Massachusetts occasional papers in linguistics 18: Papers in Optimality Theory*, 77-136. Amherst: GLSA, University of Massachusetts.

Bonet, Eulàlia
    1991   Morphology after syntax: Pronominal clitics in Romance. Ph.D.

dissertation, Department of Linguistics and Philosophy, Massachusetts Institute of Technology.

Broselow, Ellen and John McCarthy
1983   A theory of infixing reduplication. *The linguistic review* 3: 25-98.

Bruening, Benjamin
1997   Abkhaz-mabkhaz: M-reduplication in Abkhaz, weightless syllables, and base-reduplicant correspondence. In: Benjamin Bruening, Martha McGinnis, and Y. Kang (eds.), *PF: Papers at the interface. MIT Working Papers in Linguistics vol. 30.* Cambridge, Mass.: MIT Working Papers in Linguistics.

Carrier, Jill Louise
1979   The interaction of morphological and phonological rules in Tagalog. Ph.D. dissertation, Department of Linguistics and Philosophy, Massachusetts Institute Of Technology.

Chomsky, Noam
1965   *Aspects of the theory of syntax.* Cambridge, Mass.: MIT Press.
1975   *Logical structure of linguistic theory.* New York: Plenum.
1995   *The Minimalist Program.* Cambridge, Mass.: MIT Press.

Chomsky, Noam and Morris Halle
1968   *The sound pattern of English.* New York: Harper and Row.

Clements, George N.
1985   The problem of transfer in nonlinear morphology. *Cornell Working Papers in Linguistics*, 7, 38-73.

Cowper, Elizabeth and Karen Rice
1985   Phonology and reduplication. Ms. University of Toronto.

Diffolth, Gerard
1976   Expressives in Semai. In: Philip N. Jenner, Laurence C. Thompson and Stanley Starosta (eds.) *Austroasiatic Studies*, Part I. 249-264.

Emeneau, Murray
1938   An echo-word motif in Dravidian folk tales. *Journal of the American Oriental Society* 58: 553-570.

Fitzgerald, Colleen
to appear Vowel hiatus and faithfulness in Tohono O'odham reduplication. *Linguistic Inquiry* 31.4.

Frampton, John
1999   The no-crossing constraint, geminate inalterability, and reduplication. Ms. Northeastern University.

Gafos, Diamandis
1998a   A-templatic reduplication. *Linguistic Inquiry* 29: 515-527.
1998b   Eliminating long-distance consonantal spreading. *Natural language and linguistic theory*, 16: 223-278.

Goldsmith, John
1976   Autosegmental phonology. Ph.D. dissertation, Department of Linguistics and Philosophy, Massachusetts Institute Of Technology.

Halle, Morris
1998   The stress of English words 1968-1998. *Linguistic Inquiry* 29: 539-568.

Halle, Morris and William Idsardi
1997   r, hypercorrection and the elsewhere condition. In: Iggy Roca (ed.) *Derivations and constraints in phonology*, 331-348. Oxford: Clarendon Press.

to appear   Stress and length in Hixkaryana. *The Linguistic Review.*

Halle, Morris and Alec Marantz
1993   Distributive morphology and the pieces of inflection. In Kenneth Hale and Samuel Jay Keyser (eds.). *The view from building 20: Essays in honor of Sylvain Bromberger*, 111-176. Cambridge, Mass.: MIT Press.

1994   Some key features of Distributed Morphology. *MIT Working Papers in Linguistics vol. 21*: 275-288. Cambridge, Mass.: MIT Working Papers in Linguistics.

Harrison, Sheldon
1976   *Mokilese reference grammar.* Honolulu: The University Press of Hawaii.

Hayes, Bruce and May Abad
1989   Reduplication and syllabification in Ilokano. *Lingua* 77: 331-374.

Hendricks, Sean
1998   Reduplication without prosodic templates: a case from Semai. Talk presented at the Annual Meeting of the LSA, New York, 1998.

Hill, Jane H. and Ofelia Zepeda
1992   Derived words in Tohono O'odham. *International Journal of American Linguistics*, 58: 355-404.

Hyman, Larry
1990   Non-Exhaustive Syllabification: Evidence from Nigeria and Cameroon. In: Michael Ziolkowski, Manuela Noske, and Karen Deaton (eds.) *CLS 26: Papers from the parasession on the syllable in phonetics and phonology* 175-195. Chicago Linguistic Society.

Idsardi, William
1992   The computation of prosody. Ph.D. dissertation, Department of Linguistics and Philosophy, Massachusetts Institute Of Technology.

Idsardi, William and Sun-Hoi Kim
to appear   On syllable-based multiple opacities. *International Workshop on Generative Grammar*, Seoul, Korea 2000.

Idsardi, William and Eric Raimy
2000   Reduplicative economy. Ms. University of Delaware.

Inkelas, Sharon
2000   Infixation obviates backcopying in Tagalog. Talk presented at the Annual Meeting of the LSA, Chicago, 2000.

Inkelas, Sharon and Cheryl Zoll
1999 Reduplication as double stem selection. Talk presented at the Phonology 2000 Conference, Harvard University and MIT.
2000a Morphosyntactic identity and reduplication. Handout from the 1st North American Phonology Conference.
2000b Reduplication as morphological doubling. Ms. University of California, Berkeley and Massachusetts Institute of Technology. ROA 412.

International Phonetic Association
1999 *The handbook of the International Phonetic Alphabet: A guide to the use of the International Phonetic Alphabet.* Cambridge: Cambridge University Press.

Ito, Junko
1988 *Syllable theory in prosodic phonology.* New York: Garland Press.

Ito, Junko and Ralf Armin Mester
1999 On the sources of opacity in OT: Coda processes in German. Ms. University of California, Santa Cruz. ROA 347.

Jones, Caroline
1997 Contiguity under infixation: Mangarrayi reduplication. Handout from Hopkins Optimality Theory workshop, Baltimore, MD.

Kaisse, Ellen
2000 Sympathy meets Argentinean Spanish. Ms. University of Washington.

Kayne, Richard
1994 *The antisymmetry of syntax.* Cambridge, Mass.: MIT Press.

Kenstowicz, Michael
1981 Functional explanations in generative phonology. In: D. L. Goyvaerts (ed.) *Phonology in the 1980's.* Ghent: E. Story-Scientia.

Kenstowicz, Michael and Degif Petros Banksira
1999 Reduplicative identity in Chaha. *Linguistic Inquiry,* 30: 573-585.

Kiparsky, Paul
1973 'Elsewhere' in phonology. In: Stephen Anderson and Paul Kiparsky (eds.), *A Festschrift for Morris Halle,* 277-314. New York: Academic Press.
1982 Lexical phonology and morphology. In: I. S. Yang (ed.), *Linguistics in the morning calm,* 3-91. Seoul: Hanshin.
1986 The phonology of reduplication. Ms. Stanford University.
1998 Paradigm effects and opacity. Ms. Stanford University.

Kitagawa, Yoshihisa
1987 Redoing reduplication: A preliminary sketch. *Syntax and Semantics,* 20: 71-106.

Leben, William
1973 Suprasegmental phonology. Ph.D. dissertation, Department of Linguistics and Philosophy, Massachusetts Institute Of Technology.

Lee, Kee-dong
 1975   *Kusaiean reference grammar.* Honolulu: The University Press of Hawaii.
Lidz, Jeffrey
 1999   Echo reduplication in Kannada: Implications for a theory of word-formation. Ms. University of Pennsylvania
Lieber, Rochelle
 1980   On the organization of the lexicon. Ph.D. dissertation, Department of Linguistics and Philosophy, Massachusetts Institute Of Technology.
Marantz, Alec
 1982   Re reduplication. *Linguistic Inquiry,* 13: 435-482.
Martin, Samuel E.
 1992   *A reference grammar of Korean.* Rutland, Vermont: Charles E. Tuttle Company.
McCarthy, John
 1979   *Formal problems in Semitic phonology and morphology.* New York: Garland.
 1982   Prosodic templates, morphemic templates, and morphemic tiers. In: Harry van der Hulst and Norval Smith (eds.) *The structure of phonological representations, part I.* 191-224. Dordrecht: Foris.
 1999   Harmonic serialism and parallelism. Ms. University of Massachusetts. ROA 357.
 2000   Sympathy and phonological opacity. *Phonology* 16: 331-399.
McCarthy, John and Alan Prince
 1986   Prosodic morphology. Ms. Published as Technical Report #32, Center for Cognitive Sciences, Rutgers University.
 1993a   Generalized Alignment. In: Geert Booij and Jaap van Marle (eds.) *Yearbook of morphology 1993.* 79-153. Dordrecht: Kluwer.
 1993b   Prosodic morphology I: Constraint interaction and satisfaction. Ms. University of Massachusetts, Amherst and Rutgers University.
 1994a   The emergence of the unmarked: Optimality in Prosodic Morphology. In *Proceedings of the North East Linguistics Society 24*, 333-379. GLSA, University of Massachusetts, Amherst.
 1994b   Two lectures on Prosodic Morphology. The Utrecht Workshop on Prosodic Morphology. ROA 59.
 1995   Faithfulness and Reduplicative Identity. In *University of Massachusetts occasional papers in linguistics 18: Papers in Optimality Theory,* 249-384. GLSA, University of Massachusetts, Amherst.
 1997   Faithfulness and identity in Prosodic Morphology. Ms. University of Massachusetts, Amherst and Rutgers University, New Brunswick. ROA 216.
Mester, R. Armin
 1988   *Studies in tier structure.* New York: Garland.

Moravcsik, Edith
    1978   Reduplicative constructions. In: Joseph Greenberg (ed.) *Universals of human language, vol. 3*, 297-334. Stanford: Stanford University Press.

Nater, Henry
    1984   *The Bella Coola Language.* Canadian Ethnology Service Paper 92. Ottawa: Museum of Man.
    1990   *A Concise Nuxalk-English Dictionary.* Canadian Ethnology Service Paper 115. Ottawa: Museum of Civilization.

Newman, Stanley
    1971   Bella Coola reduplication. *International Journal of American Linguistics* 37: 34-38.

Noyer, Rolf
    1997   *Features, positions, and affixes in autonomous morphological structure.* New York: Garland.
    1998   Impoverishment theory and morphosyntactic markedness. In: Steven G. Lapointe, Diane K. Brentari, and Patrick M. Ferrell (eds.) *Morphology and its relation to phonology and syntax* 264-285. Stanford: CSLI Publications.

Odden, David
    2000   Ordering. Ms. Ohio State University.

Onn, Farid
    1980   *Aspects of Malay phonology and morphology: A generative approach.* Bangi: Universiti Kebangsaan Malaysia.

Perlmutter, David
    1998   Interfaces: Explanation of allomorphy and the architecture of grammars. In: Steven G. Lapointe, Diane K. Brentari and Patrick M. Farrell (eds.) *Morphology and its relation to phonology and syntax.* 307-338, Stanford: CSLI Publications.

Prince, Alan
    1977   The phonology and morphology of Tiberian Hebrew. Ph.D. dissertation, Department of Foreign Literatures and Linguistics, Massachusetts Institute of Technology.

Prince, Alan and Paul Smolensky
    1993   Optimality Theory: Constraint interaction in generative grammar. Ms. Rutgers University, New Brunswick, and University of Colorado, Boulder.

Radhakrishnan, R.
    1981   *The Nancowry word: Phonology, affixal morphology, and roots of a Nicobarese language.* Carbondale, Illinois and Edmonton, Alberta: Linguistic Research.

Raimy, Eric
    1999   Representing Reduplication. Ph.D. dissertation, University of Delaware.
    2000   Remarks on backcopying. *Linguistic Inquiry* 31: 541-552.

to appear Strong syllable reduplication in Mokilese. In: *The proceedings from ESCOL '99*, Cornell University Press.

Raimy, Eric and William Idsardi
1997   A minimalist approach to reduplication in OT. In: Kiyomi Kusumoto (ed.) *NELS 27: Proceedings of the North East Linguistics Society*, 369-382. GLSA, University of Massachusetts, Amherst.

Robins, R. H
1957   Vowel nasality in Sundanese: A phonological and grammatical study. In *Studies in linguistic analysis* (special volume, Philological Society). Oxford: Basil Blackwell.

Sagey, Elizabeth
1990   *The representation of features and relations in nonlinear phonology.* New York: Garland.

Sapir, Edward
1930   Southern Paiute, a Shoshonean language. In: William Blight (ed.), *The collected works of Edward Sapir X*, 17-314. New York: Mouton de Gruyter.
1931   Southern Paiute Dictionary. In: William Blight (ed.), *The collected works of Edward Sapir X*, 557-752. New York: Mouton de Gruyter.

Saxton, Dean, Lucille Saxton and Susie Enos
1983   *Papago/Pima-English, English-Papago/Pima Dictionary, 2nd edition.* Tucson: University of Arizona Press

Schachter, Paul and Victoria Fromkin
1968   *A phonology of Akan: Akupem, Asante & Fante.* Working Papers in Phonetics Vol. 9. University of California, Los Angeles.

Schein, Barry and Donca Steriade
1986   On geminates. *Linguistic Inquiry* 17: 691-744.

Seong, Teoh Boon
1994   *The sound system of Malay revisited.* Kuala Lumpur: Dewan Bahasa dan Pustaka, Ministry of Education Malaysia.

Shaw, Patricia
1993   The prosodic constituency of minor syllables. In *Proceedings of the Eleventh West Coast Conference on Formal Linguistics*, 117-132. Stanford: CSLI Publications.

Sloan, Kelly
1988   Bare-consonant reduplication: Implications for a prosodic theory of reduplication. In *Proceedings of the Seventh West Coast Conference on Formal Linguistics*, 319-330. Stanford: CSLI Publications.

Spaelti, Phillip
1997   Dimensions of variation in multi-pattern reduplication. Ph.D. dissertation, Department of Linguistics, University of California, Santa Cruz.

Sproat, Richard
1985   On deriving the lexicon. Ph.D. dissertation, Department of Linguistics and Philosophy, Massachusetts Institute of Technology.

Stemberger, Joseph
  1996   The scope of the theory: Where does 'beyond' lie? In: Kora Singer
            McNair, Lise M. Dobrin and Michelle M. Aucoin (eds.) *CLS 32:
            The parasession on theory and data in linguistics.* 139-164.
Steriade, Donca
  1988   Reduplication and syllable transfer in Sanskrit and elsewhere. *Pho-
            nology*, 5: 73-155.
Struijke, Caro
  1998   Reduplicant and output TETU in Kwakwala: a new model of cor-
            respondence. Ms. University of Maryland, College Park. ROA 261.
Uhrbach, Amy
  1987   A formal analysis of reduplication and its interaction with
            phonological and morphological processes. Ph.D. dissertation, De-
            partment of Linguistics, University of Texas, Austin.
Urbanczyk, Suzanne
  1996   Patterns of reduplication in Lushootseed. Ph.D. dissertation, De-
            partment of Linguistics, University of Massachusetts, Amherst.
Uriagereka, Juan
  1999   Multiple spell-out. In: Samuel D. Epstein and Norbert Hornstein
            (eds.) *Working minimalism*, 251-282. Cambridge, Mass.: MIT
            Press.
Ussishkin, Adam
  2000   The inadequacy of the consonantal root: Modern Hebrew denomi-
            nal verbs and Output-Output correspondence. *Phonology* 16: 401-
            442.
Walker, Rachel
  1998a   Minimizing RED: Nasal copy in Mbe. Ms. University of Califor-
            nia, Santa Cruz. ROA 264.
  1998b   Nasalization, neutral segments, and opacity effects. Ph.D. disserta-
            tion, University of California, Santa Cruz.
Wash, Suzanne
  1995   Productive reduplication in Barbareño Chumash. M.A. thesis. De-
            partment of Linguistics, University of California, Santa Barbara.
Wilbur, Ronnie
  1973   The phonology of reduplication. Ph.D. dissertation, Department of
            Linguistics, University of Illinois. Distributed by the Indiana Uni-
            versity Linguistics Club, Bloomington, Indiana.
Zepeda, Ofelia
  1983   *A Papago grammar.* Tucson: University of Arizona Press
Zoll, Cheryl
  1998   Positional Asymmetries and Licensing. Ms. Massachusetts Institute
            of Technology. ROA 282.
  2000   Normal application in Klamath intensive reduplication. Talk pre-
            sented at the Annual Meeting of the LSA, Chicago, 2000.

Index